"The Ultimate Guide to Making Money and Achieving Financial Independence"

Laurel D. Malvern

Copyright and Legal Disclaimer

The Ultimate Guide to Making Money and Achieving Financial Independence

© 2024 by Laurel D. Malvern. All rights reserved.

No part of this publication may be reproduced, distributed, or transmitted in any form or by any means, including photocopying, recording, or other electronic or mechanical methods, without the prior written permission of the publisher, except in the case of brief quotations embodied in critical reviews and certain other noncommercial uses permitted by copyright law.

Legal Disclaimer

The information provided in this book is for general informational purposes only. While the author has made every effort to ensure the accuracy of the information contained in this book, the content is provided "as is," without warranty of any kind, express or implied, including but not limited to the implied warranties of merchantability, fitness for a particular purpose, or non-infringement.

The strategies and advice contained herein may not be suitable for every individual, and the information provided should not be relied upon as a substitute for professional financial advice. Readers are encouraged to consult with a qualified financial advisor before making any financial decisions. The author and publisher disclaim any liability for any direct, indirect, incidental, consequential, or other damages arising out of or in connection with the use of the information presented in this book.

The author does not guarantee any specific outcomes, financial results, or success from the use of the concepts, methods, and techniques discussed in this book. Individual results may vary based on a wide range of factors, including but not limited to personal circumstances, market conditions, and adherence to the advice provided.

The trademarks, service marks, and product names mentioned in this book are the property of their respective owners. The use of these names does not imply endorsement by or affiliation with the trademark holders.

Laurel D. Malvern

"The Ultimate Guide to Making Money and Achieving Financial Independence"

Preface 7

Chapter 1: The Ultimate Guide to Making Money and Achieving Financial Independence 10

Chapter 2: Overview of Traditional vs. Modern Ways to Make Money 13

Chapter 3: The Importance of Diversified Income Streams 17

Chapter 4: Setting Financial Goals 21

Chapter 5: Foundations of Making Money Online 25

Chapter 6: Understanding the Online Economy 30

Chapter 7: Overview of the Digital Economy 35

Chapter 8: Benefits and Challenges of Making Money Online 41

Chapter 8A: Key Skills and Tools Required 46

Chapter 9: Passive Income Streams 49

Chapter 10: Definition and Benefits of Passive Income 53

Chapter 11: Examples of Passive Income Streams 57

Chapter 12: Steps to Create and Maintain Passive Income Sources 62

Chapter 13: Making Money from Home 68

Chapter 14: Overview of Work-from-Home Opportunities 73

Chapter 15: Setting Up a Productive Home Office 79

Chapter 16: Balancing Work and Home Life 85

Chapter 17: Investing for Financial Growth 90

Chapter 18: Investing for Beginners 95

Chapter 19: Basic Principles of Investing 99

Chapter 20: Types of Investments: Stocks, Bonds, Mutual Funds 103

Chapter 21: Understanding Risk and Return 107

Chapter 22: Stock Market Investing 110

Chapter 23: Personal Finance Management 113

Chapter 24: Specialized Investment Strategies 116

Chapter 25: Real Estate Investing 120

Chapter 26: Cryptocurrency Investing 124

Chapter 27: Online Business Models 128

Chapter 28: Dropshipping 133

Chapter 29: Affiliate Marketing 137

Chapter 30: Additional Income Streams 141

Chapter 31: Side Hustles 145

Chapter 32: Freelancing 149

Chapter 33: E-commerce 152

Chapter 34: Financial Independence 155

Chapter 35: Budgeting for Financial Success 158

Chapter 36: Achieving Financial Independence 162

Conclusion 166

Appendices 169

Preface

Welcome to "The Ultimate Guide to Making Money and Achieving Financial Independence." This book is the culmination of years of research, personal experience, and the insights I've gained from countless conversations with financial experts and successful individuals from various walks of life. My name is Laurel D. Malvern, and my journey towards financial independence has been both challenging and incredibly rewarding. I wrote this book to share the knowledge I've accumulated and to provide a comprehensive guide for anyone looking to take control of their financial future.

In today's fast-paced world, financial stability and independence are more crucial than ever. Whether you're just starting your career, looking to invest wisely, or planning for retirement, the principles and strategies outlined in this book are designed to help you navigate the complex world of personal finance. My goal is to empower you with the tools and confidence to make informed financial decisions that will lead to lasting success and peace of mind.

This book covers a wide range of topics, from budgeting and saving to investing and creating multiple streams of income. Each chapter is packed with practical advice, real-world examples, and actionable steps you can take immediately to improve your financial situation. I have also included tips for developing a wealth mindset, which I believe is the foundation for achieving any financial goal.

One of the key messages I hope to convey is that financial independence is not just about accumulating wealth—it's about creating a life of freedom and opportunity. It's about having the resources to pursue your passions, support your loved ones, and make a positive impact on the world. Throughout the book, you'll find stories of individuals who have transformed their lives by applying the principles discussed here. These stories serve as both inspiration and proof that achieving financial independence is possible for anyone willing to put in the effort.

I want to thank you for picking up this book and taking the first step towards a brighter financial future. Remember, the journey to financial independence is a marathon, not a sprint. Be patient, stay disciplined, and keep learning. I'm excited to be part of your journey and look forward to seeing the incredible things you will accomplish.

Here's to your success and financial freedom!

Warm regards,

Laurel D. Malvern

Chapter 1: The Ultimate Guide to Making Money and Achieving Financial Independence

Introduction
The Changing Landscape of Income Generation
In the past, the path to financial security was relatively straightforward: get a good education, secure a stable job, and save diligently. However, the economic landscape has dramatically shifted in recent decades, driven by rapid technological advancements, globalization, and evolving employment trends. Today, the traditional model of earning a single income from a lifelong job is no longer the norm, nor is it the most effective strategy for achieving financial independence.

The digital revolution has opened up countless opportunities for generating income. From remote work and freelancing to online businesses and investment platforms, individuals now have unprecedented access to diverse revenue streams. This chapter explores how these changes have redefined the ways we can earn money and set the stage for achieving financial independence.

The Gig Economy

One of the most significant developments in recent years is the rise of the gig economy. Platforms like Uber, Airbnb, and Fiverr have created a marketplace for short-term, flexible work opportunities. This shift allows individuals to monetize their skills, time, and assets in ways that were previously unimaginable. The gig economy offers a valuable source of supplemental income and, for some, a primary income stream that provides both flexibility and control over their work-life balance.

Online Entrepreneurship
The internet has democratized entrepreneurship. Starting an online business has become more accessible and affordable than ever before. Whether it's through e-commerce, digital marketing, or content creation, the online space offers numerous avenues for building a profitable business. Entrepreneurs can reach a global audience with minimal upfront costs, leveraging tools and platforms that simplify operations, marketing, and sales.

Investment Opportunities
Investment opportunities have also expanded and become more inclusive. Traditional barriers to investing, such as high entry costs and lack of access to information, are being dismantled. Today, anyone with an internet connection can participate in stock markets, real estate crowdfunding, peer-to-peer lending, and cryptocurrency trading. These options enable individuals to grow their wealth passively, complementing active income sources.

Remote Work

The COVID-19 pandemic accelerated the adoption of remote work, proving that many jobs can be performed from anywhere in the world. This shift has allowed people to explore new career opportunities without geographical limitations. Remote work not only offers flexibility but also opens up possibilities for reducing living expenses by relocating to more affordable areas.

The Importance of Multiple Income Streams
Relying on a single income source can be risky in today's volatile economic environment. Diversifying income streams is a crucial strategy for achieving financial independence. By combining active and passive income sources, individuals can create a more resilient financial foundation. This approach provides stability and increases the potential for wealth accumulation over time.

Conclusion
The changing landscape of income generation presents both challenges and opportunities. Embracing these changes requires a proactive and open-minded approach to personal finance. By leveraging the diverse income opportunities available today, you can take significant steps toward achieving financial independence. In the following chapters, we will delve deeper into specific strategies and actionable steps to help you navigate this new economic terrain and build a secure financial future.

Chapter 2: Overview of Traditional vs. Modern Ways to Make Money

In this chapter, we'll explore the contrast between traditional and modern methods of generating income. Understanding these different approaches will help you identify opportunities that best suit your skills, interests, and financial goals.

Traditional Ways to Make Money

1. Employment
Traditional employment involves working for a company or organization in exchange for a salary or hourly wage. This method provides stability, benefits, and a clear career path, but it often lacks flexibility and limits earning potential to a fixed income.

2. Small Business Ownership
Owning a small business has been a cornerstone of the traditional economy. Entrepreneurs invest capital to start and run businesses such as retail stores, restaurants, or service-based companies. While this can offer substantial rewards, it also comes with high risk and significant upfront costs.

3. Investments
Traditional investment strategies include stocks, bonds, and real estate. These methods require initial capital and a good understanding of market dynamics. Returns can be significant, but so can losses, especially without proper knowledge and strategy.

4. Professional Services
Professions such as law, medicine, and accounting have long been avenues for high earning potential. These careers require extensive education and training but can provide lucrative and stable incomes.

5. Physical Assets
Investing in physical assets like real estate, precious metals, and collectibles has been a traditional way to build wealth. These assets can appreciate over time and provide a hedge against inflation.

Modern Ways to Make Money

1. Gig Economy
Platforms like Uber, Lyft, and TaskRabbit allow individuals to offer services on a flexible, freelance basis. This model provides opportunities for quick income and flexibility but often lacks benefits and long-term security.

2. Online Businesses
The internet has opened up numerous possibilities for online entrepreneurship. E-commerce, affiliate marketing, and dropshipping are just a few examples. These businesses can be started with relatively low investment and can reach a global audience.

3. Digital Content Creation
Creating digital content such as blogs, YouTube videos, podcasts, and social media can generate income through advertising, sponsorships, and direct sales. This method leverages creativity and personal branding.

4. Remote Work

The rise of remote work allows people to work from anywhere in the world. Many companies now offer remote positions, providing flexibility and the ability to reduce living expenses by moving to more affordable locations.

5. Cryptocurrency and Blockchain
Investing in cryptocurrencies and participating in blockchain-based projects have emerged as modern investment opportunities. While highly volatile, they offer the potential for significant returns.

6. Crowdfunding and Peer-to-Peer Lending
Platforms like Kickstarter and LendingClub enable individuals to fund their projects or lend money to others for interest. These methods democratize funding and investment, allowing for more direct and diverse financial opportunities.

7. Online Education and Courses
Creating and selling online courses or offering tutoring services through platforms like Udemy and Coursera can be a profitable venture. This leverages expertise and knowledge in a scalable way.

Comparing Traditional and Modern Methods
Stability vs. Flexibility
Traditional methods often provide stability and predictability but can lack flexibility. Modern methods, while potentially less stable, offer greater flexibility and the ability to adapt to changing circumstances.

Upfront Costs
Traditional businesses and investments typically require significant upfront costs. Modern methods, particularly online ventures, often have lower entry barriers, making them accessible to a wider audience.

Income Potential
Both traditional and modern methods offer significant income potential, but modern methods often allow for scalability and reaching a global market. Traditional methods, however, can provide more consistent and long-term income streams.

Risk
Modern methods can be more volatile and uncertain, especially with investments like cryptocurrency. Traditional methods tend to be more predictable, although they also come with their own risks, particularly in uncertain economic climates.

Skills and Education
Traditional methods often require formal education and professional qualifications. Modern methods may require technical skills, digital literacy, and the ability to learn and adapt quickly.

Conclusion
Both traditional and modern ways of making money have their own advantages and challenges. The best approach depends on your personal circumstances, skills, and financial goals. By understanding the strengths and weaknesses of each method, you can make informed decisions and create a diversified strategy for achieving financial independence. In the following chapters, we'll delve deeper into specific techniques and strategies within both traditional and modern frameworks to help you build a robust and resilient financial future.

Chapter 3: The Importance of Diversified Income Streams

In an ever-changing economic landscape, relying on a single source of income can be risky. Diversifying your income streams is a powerful strategy to enhance financial security and accelerate your journey toward financial independence. In this chapter, we will explore the benefits of diversification, various types of income streams, and practical steps to create and manage multiple sources of income.

Why Diversify Your Income Streams?
1. Financial Stability and Security
Relying on one income source makes you vulnerable to unexpected changes such as job loss, economic downturns, or industry disruptions. Multiple income streams provide a safety net, ensuring you have other sources to fall back on if one fails.

2. Increased Earning Potential
Diversifying your income streams can significantly boost your overall earnings. Combining different income sources allows you to maximize your financial potential and reach your financial goals faster.

3. Flexibility and Freedom
Multiple income streams can provide greater flexibility and freedom in your life. They can reduce dependence on a single job, giving you more control over your time and career choices. This can lead to a better work-life balance and the ability to pursue passions and interests.

4. Wealth Building and Passive Income

Diversifying income often involves creating passive income sources, such as investments or royalties, which generate revenue with minimal ongoing effort. Passive income is a critical component of wealth building, allowing you to earn money even when you're not actively working.

5. Mitigating Risk

Different income streams can help mitigate financial risks. When one source is underperforming, others can compensate, providing a more stable and predictable overall income.

Types of Income Streams

1. Earned Income

This is the income you receive from working a job or running a business. It includes salaries, wages, tips, and profits from business operations.

2. Portfolio Income

Portfolio income comes from investments such as stocks, bonds, mutual funds, and real estate. This income can take the form of dividends, interest, or capital gains.

3. Passive Income

Passive income is generated with minimal ongoing effort. Common sources include rental properties, royalties from creative works, and income from businesses in which you are not actively involved.

4. Side Hustles and Freelancing

Side hustles and freelance work can supplement your main income. This might include gig economy jobs, consulting, or part-time work in areas where you have expertise.

5. Online Businesses and E-commerce

The internet offers numerous opportunities to create online businesses. This can include selling products, affiliate marketing, dropshipping, or offering digital services.

6. Intellectual Property

Income from intellectual property includes royalties from books, music, patents, and trademarks. This type of income can continue to flow long after the initial work is done.

Creating and Managing Multiple Income Streams

1. Assess Your Skills and Interests

Start by assessing your skills, interests, and available resources. Choose income streams that align with your strengths and passions, making it more likely that you will enjoy and persist in these endeavors.

2. Start Small and Scale Up

Begin with one or two additional income streams to avoid becoming overwhelmed. As you gain experience and confidence, you can gradually add more streams and scale up your efforts.

3. Leverage Technology

Use technology to your advantage. Online platforms, apps, and tools can streamline processes, automate tasks, and expand your reach, making it easier to manage multiple income sources.

4. Continuously Learn and Adapt

Stay informed about trends and changes in your chosen income streams. Continuously learning and adapting to new information will help you stay competitive and capitalize on emerging opportunities.

5. Monitor and Adjust

Regularly review your income streams to assess their performance. Be prepared to adjust your strategy, discontinue underperforming streams, and invest more in those that are thriving.

6. Build a Support Network

Surround yourself with like-minded individuals who can offer advice, support, and collaboration opportunities. Networking with others can provide valuable insights and open doors to new income sources.

Conclusion

Diversifying your income streams is a critical strategy for achieving financial independence and building long-term wealth. By creating multiple sources of income, you can enhance financial stability, increase your earning potential, and gain greater flexibility and freedom in your life. In the following chapters, we will delve deeper into specific methods for building and managing diversified income streams, providing you with practical guidance to create a robust and resilient financial future.

Chapter 4: Setting Financial Goals

Achieving financial independence begins with setting clear and attainable financial goals. These goals provide direction, motivation, and a framework for making informed decisions about your money. In this chapter, we will discuss the importance of financial goals, the types of goals you should consider, and a step-by-step process for setting and achieving them.

The Importance of Financial Goals
1. Provides Direction
Financial goals give you a clear sense of direction. They help you understand where you are going and what you need to do to get there. Without goals, your financial decisions can become aimless and disorganized.

2. Motivates Action
Having specific goals keeps you motivated. When you know what you are working towards, it is easier to stay committed and disciplined in your financial habits.

3. Facilitates Planning
Goals provide a basis for financial planning. They help you determine the steps and resources needed to achieve your desired outcomes, allowing for better budgeting, saving, and investing.

4. Measures Progress
Setting financial goals allows you to track your progress over time. You can assess whether you are on track, need to make adjustments, or have achieved a milestone worth celebrating.

Types of Financial Goals

1. Short-Term Goals

Short-term goals are those you aim to achieve within a year or less. Examples include building an emergency fund, paying off a small debt, or saving for a vacation. These goals are typically more immediate and manageable.

2. Medium-Term Goals

Medium-term goals usually span one to five years. They might include saving for a down payment on a house, funding a major purchase, or paying off significant debt. These goals require more planning and consistent effort.

3. Long-Term Goals

Long-term goals extend beyond five years and often involve larger financial ambitions. Examples include retirement savings, funding your children's education, or achieving complete financial independence. These goals necessitate long-term planning, investment, and sustained discipline.

Setting Financial Goals: A Step-by-Step Process

1. Identify Your Priorities

Start by identifying your financial priorities. Consider your values, lifestyle, and what is most important to you. This will help you determine the goals that are most meaningful and relevant.

2. Be Specific

Define your goals clearly and specifically. Instead of setting a vague goal like "save money," specify the amount you want to save and the time frame in which you want to achieve it, such as "save $5,000 in one year."

3. Make Your Goals Measurable

Ensure your goals are measurable so you can track your progress. Use concrete numbers and deadlines to quantify your goals, making it easier to evaluate your success.

4. Set Realistic and Achievable Goals

Set goals that are challenging yet attainable. Consider your current financial situation, income, and expenses to ensure your goals are realistic. Setting unattainable goals can lead to frustration and discouragement.

5. Break Down Goals into Smaller Steps

Large goals can be overwhelming, so break them down into smaller, manageable steps. For example, if your goal is to save $12,000 in a year, plan to save $1,000 each month.

6. Establish a Timeline

Create a timeline for achieving your goals. This helps you stay on track and provides a sense of urgency. Set deadlines for both the overall goal and the smaller steps leading up to it.

7. Develop an Action Plan

Outline the specific actions you need to take to reach your goals. This might include creating a budget, setting up automatic transfers to a savings account, or researching investment options. An action plan provides a clear roadmap to follow.

8. Monitor Your Progress

Regularly review your progress towards your goals. Assess whether you are on track and make adjustments as needed. Monitoring your progress keeps you accountable and allows you to celebrate milestones along the way.

9. Stay Flexible

Life is unpredictable, and your financial situation may change. Be prepared to adjust your goals and plans as necessary. Flexibility ensures you can adapt to new circumstances without losing sight of your overall objectives.

10. Celebrate Achievements

Recognize and celebrate when you achieve a financial goal. Celebrating your successes helps reinforce positive financial behaviors and motivates you to continue working towards your other goals.

Conclusion

Setting financial goals is a crucial step towards achieving financial independence. Clear, specific, and measurable goals provide direction, motivation, and a framework for making informed financial decisions. By following the steps outlined in this chapter, you can set realistic and achievable goals that align with your priorities and guide you towards a secure and prosperous financial future. In the next chapters, we will delve into the specific strategies and tools that will help you achieve these goals and build a strong financial foundation.

Chapter 5: Foundations of Making Money Online

The digital age has revolutionized the way we earn money, offering a plethora of opportunities to generate income online. From freelancing and e-commerce to content creation and investing, the internet provides various avenues to build wealth and achieve financial independence. This chapter explores the foundational elements of making money online, equipping you with the knowledge and tools to start your online income journey.

The Advantages of Making Money Online
1. Flexibility
Online income opportunities often provide unparalleled flexibility. You can work from anywhere, set your own hours, and balance multiple projects, making it easier to fit work around your lifestyle.

2. Low Start-Up Costs
Many online ventures require minimal initial investment compared to traditional businesses. This lowers the barrier to entry, allowing more people to start earning money with limited financial risk.

3. Global Reach

The internet connects you to a global audience, expanding your market far beyond local boundaries. This can significantly increase your potential customer base and income.

4. Diverse Income Streams
The online space offers a variety of income streams, from active income through freelancing and e-commerce to passive income through investments and digital products. Diversifying your income online can enhance financial stability.

Key Principles for Online Success
1. Identify Your Niche
Finding a niche is crucial for standing out in the crowded online marketplace. Identify your skills, interests, and areas of expertise, and focus on a specific market segment where you can provide unique value.

2. Build a Strong Online Presence
Establishing a robust online presence is essential for attracting clients and customers. This includes creating a professional website, maintaining active social media profiles, and engaging with your audience through content and interactions.

3. Provide Value
Successful online ventures are built on providing value to your audience. Whether through products, services, or content, ensure you are meeting the needs and solving the problems of your target market.

4. Invest in Continuous Learning

The digital landscape is constantly evolving. Stay updated with the latest trends, technologies, and best practices in your field. Continuous learning will help you adapt and remain competitive.

5. Leverage Technology

Utilize tools and platforms that streamline your operations, enhance productivity, and expand your reach. From content management systems to marketing automation, leveraging technology can boost your efficiency and effectiveness.

Popular Ways to Make Money Online

1. Freelancing

Freelancing allows you to offer your skills and services to clients on a project basis. Popular freelance categories include writing, graphic design, programming, and digital marketing. Platforms like Upwork, Freelancer, and Fiverr connect freelancers with clients worldwide.

2. E-Commerce

Starting an online store can be a lucrative venture. You can sell physical products, digital products, or dropship items. Platforms like Shopify, WooCommerce, and Etsy make it easy to set up and manage your e-commerce business.

3. Content Creation

Creating content such as blogs, YouTube videos, podcasts, and social media posts can generate income through advertising, sponsorships, and affiliate marketing. Consistently producing high-quality content helps build a loyal audience and multiple revenue streams.

4. Online Courses and Coaching

Sharing your knowledge and expertise through online courses, webinars, and coaching sessions can be highly profitable. Platforms like Udemy, Teachable, and Zoom enable you to create and deliver educational content to a global audience.

5. Investing and Trading
Online investing and trading in stocks, cryptocurrencies, and other assets can grow your wealth. Platforms like Robinhood, E*TRADE, and Coinbase provide access to various investment opportunities. It's crucial to educate yourself and manage risk effectively in this field.

6. Affiliate Marketing
Affiliate marketing involves promoting other companies' products and earning a commission on sales made through your referral links. This can be done through blogs, social media, and email marketing. Successful affiliate marketing requires building a large and engaged audience.

7. Remote Work and Telecommuting
Many companies now offer remote work opportunities, allowing you to earn a salary while working from home or anywhere with an internet connection. Websites like Remote.co and We Work Remotely list remote job openings across various industries.

Steps to Get Started
1. Assess Your Skills and Interests
Evaluate your skills, interests, and experiences to determine which online income opportunities align best with your strengths. Consider what you enjoy doing and where you can add the most value.

2. Research and Plan

Conduct thorough research on your chosen niche or industry. Understand the market demand, competition, and potential challenges. Develop a detailed plan outlining your goals, target audience, and strategies for success.

3. Create a Professional Online Presence

Build a professional website and set up social media profiles to showcase your work, products, or services. Ensure your online presence reflects your brand and appeals to your target audience.

4. Network and Collaborate

Connect with other professionals in your field through online communities, social media, and networking events. Collaborating with others can lead to new opportunities, partnerships, and valuable insights.

5. Start Small and Scale Up

Begin with manageable projects or a limited product range. Focus on delivering high-quality work and building a positive reputation. As you gain experience and confidence, gradually expand your offerings and scale up your efforts.

6. Track Your Progress and Adjust

Regularly monitor your progress and evaluate the effectiveness of your strategies. Use analytics and feedback to make informed adjustments and continuously improve your online venture.

Conclusion

Making money online offers incredible potential for financial independence, but it requires dedication, strategic planning, and continuous effort. By understanding the foundational principles and exploring various online income opportunities, you can create a diversified and resilient financial future. In the following chapters, we will dive deeper into specific online money-making methods, providing detailed guidance and actionable tips to help you succeed in the digital economy.

Chapter 6: Understanding the Online Economy

To succeed in making money online, it's essential to understand the broader context of the online economy. This chapter explores the dynamics of the digital marketplace, the key drivers of the online economy, and the factors influencing its growth and evolution. By understanding these elements, you can better navigate the digital landscape and leverage opportunities for financial success.

The Digital Marketplace
1. Global Reach
The online economy transcends geographical boundaries, allowing businesses and individuals to reach a global audience. This global reach significantly expands market potential and customer base, providing opportunities that are not constrained by location.

2. Accessibility and Convenience

The internet has made it easier for people to access products, services, and information. Online platforms provide a convenient way for consumers to shop, learn, and interact, driving the demand for digital solutions.

3. Low Barriers to Entry
Starting an online business often requires less capital compared to traditional brick-and-mortar enterprises. This accessibility has democratized entrepreneurship, enabling more people to participate in the digital economy.

Key Drivers of the Online Economy
1. Technological Advancements
Advancements in technology, including faster internet speeds, mobile devices, and cloud computing, have facilitated the growth of the online economy. These innovations have improved connectivity, accessibility, and efficiency.

2. E-commerce Growth
E-commerce has become a cornerstone of the online economy. The convenience of online shopping, along with the rise of e-commerce platforms like Amazon, Alibaba, and Shopify, has driven significant growth in this sector.

3. Digital Payments
The development of secure digital payment systems, such as PayPal, Stripe, and cryptocurrency, has made online transactions more accessible and trustworthy. These payment solutions have facilitated the expansion of online businesses.

4. Social Media and Digital Marketing
Social media platforms and digital marketing tools have transformed how businesses reach and engage with customers. Targeted advertising, influencer marketing, and content marketing are essential strategies for success in the online economy.

5. Remote Work and Gig Economy

The rise of remote work and the gig economy has contributed to the online economy's growth. Platforms like Upwork, Fiverr, and Remote.co connect freelancers with clients, providing flexible work opportunities.

Factors Influencing the Online Economy

1. Consumer Behavior

Consumer preferences and behaviors are continually evolving, influenced by convenience, access to information, and changing lifestyles. Understanding these trends is crucial for businesses to meet customer expectations and stay competitive.

2. Regulatory Environment

The regulatory landscape for the online economy is constantly changing. Policies regarding data privacy, digital taxation, and e-commerce regulations can impact how businesses operate online. Staying informed about these changes is essential for compliance and strategic planning.

3. Cybersecurity

As the online economy grows, so do concerns about cybersecurity. Protecting data and ensuring secure transactions are critical for maintaining consumer trust and business integrity.

4. Technological Disruptions

Emerging technologies such as artificial intelligence, blockchain, and the Internet of Things (IoT) are poised to disrupt the online economy further. Keeping abreast of these technological advancements can provide a competitive edge.

5. Market Competition

The digital marketplace is highly competitive, with new entrants continuously emerging. Differentiation through unique value propositions, exceptional customer service, and innovative offerings is vital for standing out in a crowded market.

Trends Shaping the Future of the Online Economy

1. Mobile Commerce (M-commerce)

The increasing use of smartphones for online shopping is driving the growth of mobile commerce. Businesses must optimize their websites and services for mobile users to capitalize on this trend.

2. Personalization and Customer Experience

Consumers increasingly expect personalized experiences. Leveraging data analytics and artificial intelligence to deliver tailored recommendations and interactions can enhance customer satisfaction and loyalty.

3. Sustainability and Ethical Practices

There is a growing demand for sustainable and ethically produced products. Businesses that prioritize social and environmental responsibility can attract and retain customers who value these principles.

4. Subscription Models

Subscription-based services are gaining popularity across various sectors, from software and entertainment to physical goods. This model provides a steady revenue stream and fosters customer loyalty.

5. Influencer and Affiliate Marketing

Influencer and affiliate marketing continue to be powerful tools for reaching target audiences. Collaborating with influencers and affiliates can amplify brand visibility and drive sales.

Navigating the Online Economy

1. Research and Market Analysis

Conduct thorough research and market analysis to understand your niche, target audience, and competition. This knowledge will inform your business strategy and help you identify opportunities.

2. Build a Strong Digital Presence

Establish a professional and engaging online presence through a well-designed website, active social media profiles, and consistent branding. Your digital presence is your storefront in the online economy.

3. Leverage Data and Analytics

Utilize data and analytics tools to gain insights into customer behavior, website performance, and marketing effectiveness. Data-driven decisions can enhance your strategy and improve outcomes.

4. Invest in Cybersecurity

Prioritize cybersecurity to protect your business and customers. Implement robust security measures, such as encryption, secure payment gateways, and regular security audits.

5. Stay Agile and Adaptable

The online economy is dynamic and rapidly evolving. Stay agile and adaptable, continuously learning and adjusting your strategies to keep pace with changes and capitalize on new opportunities.

Conclusion

Understanding the online economy is crucial for successfully making money online. By grasping the key drivers, influential factors, and emerging trends, you can navigate the digital landscape more effectively and leverage opportunities for financial growth. In the subsequent chapters, we will delve into specific strategies and practical tips for building and managing successful online ventures, helping you harness the full potential of the online economy for your financial independence.

Chapter 7: Overview of the Digital Economy

The digital economy represents a vast and rapidly evolving ecosystem that encompasses all economic activities conducted through digital technologies. This chapter provides a comprehensive overview of the digital economy, highlighting its key components, driving forces, and the profound impact it has on businesses and individuals.

Defining the Digital Economy
1. Scope and Components
The digital economy includes all economic activities that result from billions of online connections among people, businesses, devices, data, and processes. Key components include:

E-commerce: Online buying and selling of goods and services.
Digital Services: Services delivered via digital platforms, such as streaming, cloud computing, and online education.
Digital Marketing: Online advertising and marketing strategies.

Financial Technology (FinTech): Digital financial services, including online banking, cryptocurrency, and mobile payments.

Gig Economy: Short-term, flexible jobs facilitated by digital platforms.

2. Characteristics

The digital economy is characterized by:

Global Reach: Ability to operate and reach customers worldwide.

Instant Communication: Real-time interactions and transactions.

Data-Driven: Heavy reliance on data for decision-making and personalization.

Innovation: Continuous technological advancements and innovations.

Driving Forces of the Digital Economy

1. Technological Advancements

Rapid advancements in technology, such as the internet, smartphones, and artificial intelligence, have been the primary drivers of the digital economy. These technologies enhance connectivity, efficiency, and innovation.

2. Consumer Behavior

Consumers' increasing preference for online shopping, digital content, and on-demand services fuels the growth of the digital economy. Convenience, speed, and personalization are key factors driving this shift.

3. Business Transformation

Businesses are adopting digital tools and strategies to improve operations, reach new markets, and enhance customer experiences. Digital transformation is essential for staying competitive in today's market.

4. Government Policies and Regulations

Governments worldwide are developing policies to support digital infrastructure, cybersecurity, and e-commerce. Regulations around data privacy, intellectual property, and digital taxation also shape the digital economy.

Key Sectors of the Digital Economy
1. E-commerce
E-commerce is a major component of the digital economy, encompassing retail, wholesale, and direct-to-consumer sales conducted online. Platforms like Amazon, Alibaba, and eBay dominate this space.

2. Digital Services
This sector includes a wide range of services provided over the internet, such as:

Streaming Services: Netflix, Spotify, and YouTube.
Cloud Computing: Amazon Web Services (AWS), Microsoft Azure, and Google Cloud.
Online Education: Coursera, Udemy, and Khan Academy.
3. FinTech
FinTech involves using technology to provide financial services, including:

Online Banking: Digital-only banks like Chime and Revolut.
Payment Solutions: PayPal, Square, and mobile payment apps like Venmo.
Cryptocurrency: Bitcoin, Ethereum, and blockchain technology.
4. Digital Marketing
Digital marketing uses online platforms to promote products and services. Key elements include:

Social Media Marketing: Facebook, Instagram, and Twitter.
Search Engine Optimization (SEO): Enhancing visibility on search engines.

Content Marketing: Blogs, videos, and infographics.
Email Marketing: Direct communication with consumers via email campaigns.

5. Gig Economy

The gig economy consists of short-term, freelance, and contract work facilitated by digital platforms such as:

Ride-Sharing: Uber and Lyft.
Freelance Services: Upwork, Fiverr, and TaskRabbit.
Delivery Services: DoorDash, Instacart, and Postmates.

Impact of the Digital Economy

1. Business Operations

Digital technologies streamline business operations, reduce costs, and improve efficiency. Automation, data analytics, and cloud services enable businesses to operate more effectively and scale quickly.

2. Employment

The digital economy has created new job opportunities and flexible working arrangements. However, it also presents challenges, such as job displacement due to automation and the need for new skill sets.

3. Consumer Experience

Consumers benefit from the convenience, variety, and personalized experiences offered by digital platforms. The ability to compare prices, read reviews, and access products and services globally enhances consumer satisfaction.

4. Innovation and Entrepreneurship

The digital economy fosters innovation and entrepreneurship by lowering barriers to entry and providing access to global markets. Startups and small businesses can compete with established companies through digital platforms.

5. Global Connectivity

Digital technologies connect people and businesses worldwide, facilitating international trade and collaboration. This global connectivity promotes economic growth and cultural exchange.

Challenges in the Digital Economy

1. Cybersecurity

As the digital economy grows, so do cybersecurity threats. Protecting data and ensuring secure transactions are critical challenges that require robust security measures and policies.

2. Data Privacy

The collection and use of personal data raise concerns about privacy. Regulations like the General Data Protection Regulation (GDPR) aim to protect consumer data, but businesses must navigate complex compliance requirements.

3. Digital Divide

Access to digital technologies is not evenly distributed, leading to a digital divide. Bridging this gap is essential for ensuring that all individuals and communities can participate in the digital economy.

4. Regulatory Compliance

Navigating the regulatory landscape can be complex for businesses operating in multiple countries. Compliance with local laws, such as digital taxation and consumer protection, is crucial for legal and ethical operations.

5. Market Competition

The digital economy is highly competitive, with rapid technological advancements and new entrants constantly emerging. Businesses must innovate continuously to stay relevant and competitive.

Conclusion

The digital economy offers immense opportunities for businesses and individuals to generate income, innovate, and connect globally. Understanding its key components, driving forces, and impact is essential for navigating this dynamic landscape successfully. In the following chapters, we will explore specific strategies and practical tips for leveraging the digital economy to build and grow your online ventures, ultimately contributing to your financial independence.

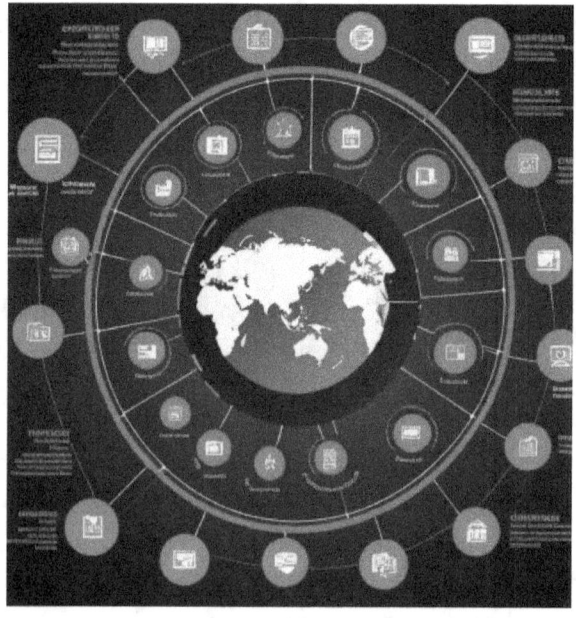

Chapter 8: Benefits and Challenges of Making Money Online

The internet has transformed the way we earn money, offering a wealth of opportunities and conveniences. However, like any venture, making money online comes with its own set of benefits and challenges. Understanding these can help you navigate the digital landscape more effectively and make informed decisions about your online income strategies.

Benefits of Making Money Online
1. Flexibility and Convenience
One of the most significant advantages of making money online is the flexibility it offers. You can work from anywhere with an internet connection, whether that's your home, a café, or while traveling. This flexibility allows you to create a work schedule that suits your lifestyle and commitments.

2. Low Start-Up Costs

Many online income opportunities require minimal initial investment compared to traditional businesses. For instance, starting a blog, becoming a freelancer, or opening an online store can be done with a small budget, making it accessible to a broader range of people.

3. Diverse Income Streams

The digital economy provides numerous ways to generate income. From e-commerce and freelancing to affiliate marketing and online courses, you can diversify your income streams to create financial stability and reduce reliance on a single source of income.

4. Global Market Reach

The internet connects you to a global audience, vastly expanding your potential market. This is particularly beneficial for e-commerce businesses and digital products, where you can sell to customers around the world without the limitations of a physical storefront.

5. Scalability

Online businesses often have greater scalability compared to traditional businesses. Digital products, for example, can be duplicated infinitely at no additional cost. With the right strategies, your online income can grow exponentially.

6. Passive Income Potential

Many online ventures offer the possibility of generating passive income. For example, creating and selling digital products, running a monetized blog, or investing in dividend-paying stocks can provide ongoing revenue with minimal active effort after the initial setup.

7. Continuous Learning and Growth

Working online often involves staying up-to-date with the latest trends, technologies, and market shifts. This continuous learning not only helps you grow your business but also enhances your personal and professional skills.

Challenges of Making Money Online

1. Competition

The online marketplace is highly competitive, with countless individuals and businesses vying for attention. Standing out requires a unique value proposition, consistent effort, and strategic marketing to attract and retain customers.

2. Uncertainty and Instability

The digital economy can be volatile. Market trends, algorithms, and consumer behavior can change rapidly, affecting your income streams. It's essential to stay adaptable and resilient in the face of these changes.

3. Technical Challenges

Navigating the technical aspects of running an online business can be daunting, especially for those without a background in technology. Building a website, managing digital marketing, and ensuring cybersecurity are critical tasks that may require learning new skills or hiring experts.

4. Self-Discipline and Time Management

Working online offers flexibility, but it also requires a high level of self-discipline and effective time management. Without the structure of a traditional job, it can be challenging to stay focused and productive, especially with the distractions of home life.

5. Isolation

Online work can be isolating, as it often involves working alone for extended periods. This lack of social interaction can lead to feelings of loneliness and disconnection. Finding ways to connect with peers, such as joining online communities or attending networking events, can help mitigate this challenge.

6. Income Fluctuations
Online income can be inconsistent, especially for freelancers and entrepreneurs. Fluctuating workloads, seasonal trends, and economic downturns can impact earnings. Building a financial cushion and diversifying income streams can help manage these fluctuations.

7. Legal and Regulatory Compliance
Operating an online business requires compliance with various legal and regulatory standards. This includes data protection laws, taxation, intellectual property rights, and consumer protection regulations. Staying informed and compliant can be complex and time-consuming.

8. Cybersecurity Risks
With the rise of the digital economy comes an increase in cybersecurity threats. Protecting your online assets, personal information, and customer data from cyber attacks is crucial. Implementing robust security measures and staying vigilant can help safeguard your online ventures.

Navigating the Benefits and Challenges
1. Develop a Solid Plan
Creating a comprehensive business plan can help you navigate the benefits and challenges of making money online. Outline your goals, target audience, revenue streams, and strategies for growth. A clear plan provides direction and helps you stay focused.

2. Continuous Learning and Adaptation

The digital landscape is constantly evolving. Stay updated with industry trends, new technologies, and best practices. Invest in continuous learning to enhance your skills and adapt to changes, ensuring long-term success.

3. Build a Strong Network

Networking with other online entrepreneurs, joining industry groups, and participating in online forums can provide valuable support, insights, and opportunities. Building a strong professional network can help you overcome challenges and grow your business.

4. Diversify Your Income Streams

Relying on a single income source can be risky. Diversify your online income streams to create financial stability and reduce vulnerability to market fluctuations. Explore various opportunities, such as freelancing, digital products, and investments.

5. Prioritize Self-Care

Balancing online work with personal well-being is essential. Establish a healthy work-life balance, take regular breaks, and prioritize self-care to prevent burnout. Staying physically and mentally healthy will enhance your productivity and overall success.

Conclusion

Making money online offers unparalleled opportunities for financial independence and personal growth. By understanding and navigating the benefits and challenges, you can build a successful and sustainable online venture. Embrace the flexibility, innovation, and potential of the digital economy, and take proactive steps to overcome obstacles and achieve your financial goals. In the following chapters, we will delve deeper into specific strategies and actionable tips for maximizing your online income and securing your financial future.

Chapter 8A: Key Skills and Tools Required

In this chapter, we delve into the essential skills and tools that will equip you on your journey to financial independence. Mastering these skills and leveraging the right tools can significantly enhance your ability to manage finances, grow wealth, and achieve your financial goals.

1. Financial Literacy

Understanding basic financial concepts is the foundation of financial independence. Key areas to focus on include:

Budgeting: Track income and expenses to ensure you live within your means.
Saving: Prioritize saving a portion of your income for emergencies and future investments.
Investing: Learn about different investment vehicles like stocks, bonds, mutual funds, and real estate.

2. Analytical Skills

Being able to analyze financial statements and market trends is crucial. This includes:

Interpreting Financial Reports: Understand balance sheets, income statements, and cash flow statements.
Market Analysis: Stay informed about market conditions and how they impact your investments.

3. Strategic Planning

Create and follow a financial plan that aligns with your goals. This involves:

Goal Setting: Define clear, measurable financial goals.
Action Plans: Develop step-by-step strategies to achieve these goals.
Risk Management: Identify potential risks and have strategies to mitigate them.

4. Discipline and Patience

Achieving financial independence is a long-term endeavor. Key attributes to cultivate are:

Consistency: Regularly contribute to savings and investment accounts.
Resilience: Stay committed to your plan even during market downturns.
Delayed Gratification: Forego immediate pleasures for long-term financial gains.

5. Networking and Mentorship
Building relationships with like-minded individuals and seeking advice from experienced mentors can provide valuable insights and opportunities.

Tools for Financial Independence
1. Budgeting Tools
Mint: A popular app that helps track spending, create budgets, and monitor financial goals.
YNAB (You Need A Budget): Focuses on proactive budgeting to ensure every dollar is assigned a job.
2. Investment Platforms
Robinhood: User-friendly for beginners, offering commission-free trades on stocks and ETFs.
Vanguard: Known for its low-cost index funds and ETFs, suitable for long-term investors.
E*TRADE: Provides a wide range of investment options and educational resources.
3. Retirement Planning Tools
Fidelity Retirement Calculator: Helps estimate how much you need to save for retirement.
Personal Capital: Offers tools to track retirement accounts and analyze investments.
4. Financial Management Software
Quicken: Comprehensive software for managing all aspects of personal finances.
QuickBooks: Ideal for those who manage small businesses in addition to personal finances.
5. Educational Resources
Coursera and Udemy: Offer courses on financial literacy, investing, and more.
Books and Podcasts: Regularly read books like "Rich Dad Poor Dad" by Robert Kiyosaki and listen to financial podcasts to stay informed.
Practical Tips for Using These Skills and Tools

Regularly Review and Adjust Your Budget: Monthly reviews help keep your finances on track.

Diversify Investments: Spread investments across different asset classes to reduce risk.

Automate Savings and Investments: Set up automatic transfers to savings and investment accounts to ensure consistent contributions.

Stay Educated: Continuously update your knowledge about financial markets and personal finance strategies.

Consult with Financial Advisors: Seek professional advice for complex financial decisions and retirement planning.

By honing these skills and utilizing the right tools, you can effectively manage your finances, make informed investment decisions, and steadily work towards achieving financial independence.

Chapter 9: Passive Income Streams

In this chapter, we explore the concept of passive income, its importance in achieving financial independence, and various strategies to generate it. Passive income allows you to earn money with minimal ongoing effort, providing a steady cash flow that supports your financial goals.

Understanding Passive Income

Passive Income vs. Active Income

Active Income: Earned from direct involvement in work, such as salaries, wages, and freelance projects.

Passive Income: Earned with little to no daily effort, such as rental income, dividends, and royalties.

Benefits of Passive Income

Financial Freedom: Reduces reliance on active income, providing more time and freedom.

Wealth Building: Enables continuous wealth accumulation even when not actively working.

Security: Creates additional income streams that can support you during economic downturns or job loss.

Popular Passive Income Streams

Real Estate Investments

Rental Properties: Purchase residential or commercial properties and earn rental income.

Real Estate Investment Trusts (REITs): Invest in REITs, which own and manage income-generating properties.

Crowdfunding Platforms: Participate in real estate crowdfunding for a share in rental income and property appreciation.

Dividend Stocks

High-Yield Stocks: Invest in companies that pay regular dividends, providing a steady income.

Dividend Growth Investing: Focus on companies with a history of increasing dividends, combining income with capital appreciation.

Peer-to-Peer Lending

Lending Platforms: Use platforms like Prosper or LendingClub to lend money to individuals or small businesses in exchange for interest payments.

Creating Digital Products

E-Books: Write and publish e-books on platforms like Amazon Kindle Direct Publishing.

Online Courses: Develop and sell online courses on platforms like Udemy or Teachable.

Stock Photos and Videos: Sell stock photos and videos on sites like Shutterstock or Adobe Stock.

Affiliate Marketing

Blogging: Create a blog and promote products or services, earning commissions for sales generated through your affiliate links.

YouTube and Social Media: Use social media channels to review and recommend products, earning affiliate commissions.

Royalties

Intellectual Property: Earn royalties from books, music, patents, or inventions.

Licensing: License your creations or intellectual property to others for ongoing income.

Automated Online Businesses

E-commerce Stores: Set up dropshipping or print-on-demand stores that require minimal management.

Subscription Services: Create subscription-based services that provide regular income from subscribers.

Investment Funds

Index Funds and ETFs: Invest in index funds and exchange-traded funds that pay dividends and appreciate over time.

Bond Funds: Invest in bond funds that provide regular interest payments.

Strategies to Build Passive Income

Start Small and Scale Up

Begin with one or two passive income streams and gradually diversify.

Reinvest earnings to grow your passive income portfolio.

Leverage Technology

Utilize online platforms and automation tools to manage passive income streams efficiently.

Use financial management apps to track and optimize income.

Educate Yourself

Continuously learn about different passive income opportunities and investment strategies.

Read books, take courses, and follow industry experts to stay informed.

Network with Like-Minded Individuals

Join communities and forums focused on passive income and financial independence.

Share experiences and learn from others' successes and challenges.

Diversify Income Streams

Avoid relying on a single source of passive income to reduce risk.

Spread investments across various assets and income-generating opportunities.

Monitor and Adjust

Regularly review the performance of your passive income streams.

Adjust strategies and investments based on market conditions and personal goals.

Practical Tips for Implementing Passive Income Strategies

Set Clear Goals: Define what you want to achieve with your passive income, such as a specific monthly income target or long-term financial security.

Research Thoroughly: Investigate each potential income stream, including risks, rewards, and required investments.

Create a Plan: Develop a step-by-step plan to start and grow your passive income streams.

Stay Committed: Building passive income takes time and effort initially; remain patient and persistent.

Seek Professional Advice: Consult financial advisors or experts when needed, especially for complex investments.

By understanding and implementing these passive income strategies, you can create multiple streams of income that support your journey to financial independence.

Chapter 10: Definition and Benefits of Passive Income

In this chapter, we define passive income in detail and explore its numerous benefits. Understanding the nature of passive income and its advantages is crucial for anyone looking to achieve financial independence and create a sustainable financial future.

What is Passive Income?
Passive Income Defined
Passive income is earnings derived from ventures in which an individual is not actively involved on a daily basis. Unlike active income, which requires continuous effort and time (such as a job or freelance work), passive income is generated with minimal ongoing involvement.

Examples of Passive Income

Dividends from stocks
Interest from savings accounts, bonds, or peer-to-peer lending
Rental income from real estate
Royalties from intellectual property such as books, music, or patents
Income from business investments where you are not actively involved
Characteristics of Passive Income
Minimal Active Involvement

Requires upfront effort to set up.
Ongoing maintenance is limited compared to active income sources.
Scalability

Potential to grow over time with reinvestment and market growth.
Can create multiple passive income streams to diversify and increase earnings.
Residual Income

Continues to generate money after the initial work is completed.
Provides a steady stream of income over time.

Benefits of Passive Income

1. Financial Freedom

Passive income is a key component of financial independence. It allows you to:

Reduce Reliance on Active Income: Decrease dependency on a traditional job.
Achieve Financial Goals Faster: Accelerate wealth accumulation and reach financial milestones more quickly.
Flexibility in Lifestyle Choices: Enjoy more time for personal pursuits, hobbies, and family.

2. Wealth Building

Passive income contributes significantly to long-term wealth:

Compound Growth: Reinvesting passive income can lead to exponential growth.
Diversification: Multiple streams of passive income diversify financial risks.

3. Security and Stability

Having passive income streams enhances financial security:

Safety Net: Provides a financial cushion during economic downturns or job loss.
Consistent Cash Flow: Offers a reliable income source regardless of employment status.

4. Increased Time Freedom

With passive income, you can:

Pursue Other Interests: Spend more time on activities you are passionate about.
Focus on Higher Goals: Engage in entrepreneurial ventures, philanthropy, or other high-impact activities without worrying about immediate financial needs.

5. Stress Reduction

Knowing that you have a continuous income stream can significantly reduce financial stress and anxiety:

Less Financial Pressure: Eases the burden of living paycheck to paycheck.
Better Quality of Life: Improves overall well-being and mental health.

Real-Life Examples of Passive Income Benefits

Case Study 1: Rental Income

Jane invests in a rental property that generates monthly rental income. After the initial purchase and setup, her ongoing efforts are limited to occasional property maintenance and management. The rental income not only covers the property's mortgage but also provides Jane with a steady additional income stream, enabling her to save more for retirement and reduce her work hours.

Case Study 2: Dividend Investing

John builds a diversified portfolio of dividend-paying stocks. Over time, the dividends provide a significant portion of his income, allowing him to reinvest a portion of the dividends to further grow his portfolio. Eventually, John achieves financial independence, supported by the passive income from his investments.

Case Study 3: Digital Products

Maria creates and sells online courses on a subject she is passionate about. After the initial work of creating the courses, her ongoing efforts are minimal, focusing mainly on marketing and occasional updates. The passive income from course sales allows Maria to travel and spend more time with her family, without worrying about financial stability.

Practical Steps to Start Building Passive Income
Identify Opportunities: Assess your interests, skills, and resources to determine suitable passive income streams.
Educate Yourself: Learn about the chosen passive income methods through courses, books, and expert advice.
Start Small: Begin with manageable investments or projects and scale up as you gain experience.
Diversify: Develop multiple passive income streams to mitigate risk and increase overall income.
Monitor and Adjust: Regularly review your passive income sources and make necessary adjustments to optimize performance.
By understanding the definition and benefits of passive income, you can strategically plan to incorporate it into your financial strategy, paving the way towards greater financial freedom and security.

Chapter 11: Examples of Passive Income Streams

In this chapter, we explore various passive income streams in detail. Understanding the different ways to generate passive income will help you diversify your sources of earnings and build a robust financial foundation.

1. Real Estate Investments
1.1 Rental Properties

Description: Purchase residential or commercial properties and rent them out.
How it Works: Tenants pay monthly rent, providing a steady income stream.
Pros: Potential for property appreciation, tax benefits.
Cons: Requires significant upfront investment, property management responsibilities.
1.2 Real Estate Investment Trusts (REITs)

Description: Invest in companies that own, operate, or finance income-producing real estate.
How it Works: Purchase shares of a REIT, which pays dividends to investors from rental income.
Pros: Lower entry cost compared to buying properties, diversified portfolio.
Cons: Subject to market risks, less control over specific properties.
1.3 Crowdfunding Platforms

Description: Participate in real estate crowdfunding platforms.
How it Works: Pool money with other investors to fund real estate projects, earning a share of the profits.

Pros: Access to large real estate projects with smaller investments, passive nature.
Cons: Illiquidity, platform fees, and potential project risks.

2. Financial Investments

2.1 Dividend Stocks

Description: Invest in stocks of companies that pay regular dividends.
How it Works: Earn dividends periodically based on the company's profits.
Pros: Potential for capital appreciation, regular income.
Cons: Market volatility, requires stock market knowledge.

2.2 Bonds

Description: Invest in bonds issued by governments or corporations.
How it Works: Earn interest payments periodically until the bond matures.
Pros: Lower risk compared to stocks, predictable income.
Cons: Lower returns, interest rate risk.

2.3 Mutual Funds and ETFs

Description: Invest in mutual funds or exchange-traded funds that focus on dividend-paying stocks or bonds.
How it Works: Pool resources with other investors to buy a diversified portfolio managed by professionals.
Pros: Diversification, professional management.
Cons: Management fees, market risk.

2.4 Peer-to-Peer Lending

Description: Lend money to individuals or small businesses through online platforms.
How it Works: Earn interest on the loans you provide.
Pros: Higher returns compared to traditional savings accounts, helping borrowers.
Cons: Credit risk, platform fees, and potential defaults.

3. Business and Digital Products

3.1 Creating Digital Products

E-Books: Write and publish e-books on platforms like Amazon Kindle.
Online Courses: Develop and sell courses on platforms like Udemy or Teachable.
Stock Photos and Videos: Sell on sites like Shutterstock or Adobe Stock.
How it Works: Create once, earn royalties or sales income repeatedly.
Pros: Low ongoing effort, scalability.
Cons: Initial time investment, competition.

3.2 Affiliate Marketing

Description: Promote products or services and earn commissions for sales through your affiliate links.
How it Works: Use blogs, YouTube channels, or social media to recommend products.
Pros: Low startup costs, can be integrated into existing content platforms.
Cons: Requires traffic and audience, commission rates vary.

3.3 Automated Online Businesses

E-commerce Stores: Set up dropshipping or print-on-demand stores.
Subscription Services: Offer subscription-based content or products.
How it Works: Use automated systems to handle sales, inventory, and shipping.
Pros: Can operate 24/7, scalability.
Cons: Initial setup effort, requires marketing skills.

4. Intellectual Property

4.1 Royalties from Creative Works

Books: Write and publish books to earn royalties from sales.

Music: Compose music and earn royalties from sales, streaming, or performance rights.
Patents: License inventions to companies and earn royalties.
How it Works: Create intellectual property that generates income over time.
Pros: Long-term income potential, can be highly lucrative.
Cons: Initial creative effort, legal protection required.

5. Miscellaneous

5.1 High-Yield Savings Accounts and CDs

Description: Deposit money in high-yield savings accounts or certificates of deposit.
How it Works: Earn interest on your deposits.
Pros: Low risk, FDIC insured.
Cons: Lower returns compared to other investments.

5.2 Cashback and Rewards Programs

Description: Earn cashback or rewards from credit card purchases and loyalty programs.
How it Works: Use credit cards or participate in programs that offer cashback or rewards points.
Pros: Easy to integrate into daily spending, additional perks.
Cons: Requires disciplined spending to avoid debt, rewards may be limited.

Practical Tips for Building Passive Income Streams

Start Small and Expand: Begin with one or two manageable income streams and gradually diversify as you gain experience and resources.
Leverage Technology: Use tools and platforms that automate tasks, such as property management software, investment apps, and e-commerce platforms.
Educate Yourself: Continuously learn about different passive income opportunities and stay updated on market trends.
Network and Collaborate: Join communities, forums, and networking groups to share experiences and gain insights from others.

Reinvest Earnings: Use the income generated from passive streams to reinvest in other opportunities, compounding your earnings over time.

By exploring and implementing these passive income streams, you can create a diversified portfolio of earnings that supports your financial independence and enhances your long-term financial security.

Chapter 12: Steps to Create and Maintain Passive Income Sources

In this chapter, we provide a step-by-step guide to creating and maintaining passive income sources. Building passive income streams requires careful planning, consistent effort, and strategic management. Follow these steps to set up and sustain your passive income ventures successfully.

Step 1: Assess Your Financial Situation and Goals
1.1 Evaluate Your Current Finances

Net Worth Assessment: Calculate your assets and liabilities to understand your starting point.
Budget Review: Analyze your income, expenses, and savings to identify how much you can invest in passive income opportunities.
1.2 Set Clear Financial Goals

Short-Term Goals: Define what you want to achieve within the next 1-2 years (e.g., save $10,000, generate $500/month in passive income).
Long-Term Goals: Establish long-term objectives (e.g., financial independence, retire by age 50).
Step 2: Research and Choose Passive Income Streams
2.1 Explore Different Options

Real Estate: Rental properties, REITs, crowdfunding.
Investments: Dividend stocks, bonds, mutual funds, ETFs.
Digital Products: E-books, online courses, stock photos.
Business Models: Affiliate marketing, automated online stores, subscription services.
Intellectual Property: Royalties from books, music, patents.

2.2 Evaluate Suitability and Risk

Risk Tolerance: Understand your risk appetite and choose income streams accordingly.
Time Commitment: Consider the initial and ongoing time investment required.
Financial Investment: Assess the capital needed to start and maintain each income stream.

2.3 Seek Advice and Insights

Mentorship: Connect with experienced individuals in your chosen fields.
Online Communities: Join forums and groups focused on passive income and financial independence.
Professional Advice: Consult financial advisors or experts if necessary.

Step 3: Create a Detailed Plan

3.1 Develop an Action Plan

Timeline: Set specific milestones and deadlines for each step.
Resources: Identify the tools, platforms, and resources needed.
Budget: Allocate funds for initial investments, marketing, and ongoing expenses.

3.2 Set Up the Chosen Income Streams

Real Estate: Purchase properties, invest in REITs, or join crowdfunding platforms.
Investments: Open brokerage accounts, buy dividend-paying stocks or bonds.
Digital Products: Create content, set up sales platforms, and market your products.
Business Models: Establish websites, join affiliate programs, and automate operations.

Step 4: Monitor and Manage Your Income Streams

4.1 Regularly Review Performance

Financial Tracking: Use financial management software to track income, expenses, and returns.

Performance Metrics: Monitor key indicators such as occupancy rates for rental properties, dividend yields, and sales figures for digital products.

4.2 Make Necessary Adjustments

Rebalance Portfolio: Adjust your investments based on market conditions and performance.

Optimize Operations: Improve efficiency and profitability through better management and marketing strategies.

Expand and Diversify: As you gain experience, reinvest earnings into new passive income opportunities.

4.3 Stay Informed and Educated

Continuous Learning: Keep up with industry trends, market developments, and new technologies.

Professional Development: Take courses, attend seminars, and read relevant books and articles.

Step 5: Automate and Delegate

5.1 Leverage Technology

Automation Tools: Use software and apps to automate tasks such as investment rebalancing, property management, and online sales.

Scheduling Systems: Implement automated scheduling for content publishing, email marketing, and social media.

5.2 Delegate Tasks

Outsource: Hire freelancers or agencies for tasks such as website management, content creation, and customer service.

Property Management: Use professional property management services for rental properties.

Step 6: Reinvest and Scale Up

6.1 Reinvest Earnings

Compounding Growth: Reinvest income to buy more assets, improve existing ones, or diversify into new opportunities.
Long-Term Planning: Focus on sustainable growth and building a diversified portfolio.

6.2 Scale Up Operations

Expand Reach: Increase marketing efforts, launch new products, or enter new markets.
Optimize Strategies: Continuously improve your strategies based on performance data and market feedback.

Step 7: Plan for Sustainability

7.1 Risk Management

Emergency Fund: Maintain a reserve fund to cover unexpected expenses or downturns.
Insurance: Protect your assets with appropriate insurance coverage.

7.2 Exit Strategy

Succession Planning: Prepare for the future by planning how to transfer or sell your income streams.
Retirement Planning: Align your passive income strategy with your retirement goals.

Practical Tips for Success

Start Early and Be Patient: Building passive income takes time. Start as soon as possible and be patient with the process.
Diversify Income Streams: Avoid relying on a single source of passive income to reduce risk and increase stability.
Stay Disciplined: Regularly review and stick to your financial plan, making adjustments as needed.
Seek Continuous Improvement: Always look for ways to optimize and enhance your passive income strategies.
Maintain a Balanced Approach: Balance risk and reward by diversifying across different types of passive income streams.

By following these steps, you can effectively create and maintain passive income sources that support your journey towards financial independence and long-term wealth.

Chapter 13: Making Money from Home

In this chapter, we explore various ways to earn money from the comfort of your home. Whether you are looking to supplement your income or establish a full-time home-based business, the following opportunities provide flexible and potentially lucrative options.

1. Freelancing
1.1 Writing and Editing

Description: Offer writing, proofreading, and editing services.
Platforms: Upwork, Fiverr, Freelancer, ProBlogger.
Skills Needed: Strong command of language, attention to detail, ability to meet deadlines.
Examples: Content creation, copywriting, blog posts, technical writing.
1.2 Graphic Design

Description: Create visual content for clients.
Platforms: 99designs, DesignCrowd, Dribbble, Behance.
Skills Needed: Proficiency in design software (Adobe Creative Suite), creativity, understanding of branding.
Examples: Logos, marketing materials, social media graphics.
1.3 Web Development

Description: Design and develop websites and web applications.
Platforms: Upwork, Toptal, GitHub Jobs.
Skills Needed: Coding languages (HTML, CSS, JavaScript, etc.), understanding of UX/UI principles.

Examples: Building websites, developing custom web applications, website maintenance.

2. Online Teaching and Tutoring

2.1 Online Courses

Description: Create and sell online courses on various subjects.
Platforms: Udemy, Teachable, Coursera.
Skills Needed: Expertise in a specific subject, ability to create engaging content.
Examples: Language learning, coding, digital marketing, personal development.

2.2 Tutoring

Description: Provide one-on-one or group tutoring sessions.
Platforms: Chegg Tutors, Wyzant, Tutor.com.
Skills Needed: Proficiency in subject matter, communication skills, patience.
Examples: Academic subjects, test preparation, skill development.

3. E-Commerce

3.1 Dropshipping

Description: Sell products without holding inventory by partnering with suppliers.
Platforms: Shopify, WooCommerce, Oberlo.
Skills Needed: Marketing, customer service, understanding of e-commerce platforms.
Examples: Niche products, branded merchandise, trending items.

3.2 Print on Demand

Description: Create custom designs for products like t-shirts, mugs, and phone cases.
Platforms: Printful, Printify, Redbubble, Teespring.

Skills Needed: Graphic design, marketing, understanding of e-commerce.
Examples: Custom apparel, home decor, accessories.

3.3 Handmade Goods

Description: Sell handmade or customized products.
Platforms: Etsy, Handmade at Amazon, ArtFire.
Skills Needed: Craftsmanship, creativity, marketing.
Examples: Jewelry, artwork, personalized gifts.

4. Remote Work

4.1 Virtual Assistance

Description: Provide administrative support to businesses or entrepreneurs.
Platforms: Belay, Time Etc, Zirtual.
Skills Needed: Organizational skills, communication, proficiency in office software.
Examples: Scheduling, email management, bookkeeping, customer support.

4.2 Customer Service

Description: Handle customer inquiries and support via phone, chat, or email.
Platforms: LiveOps, Arise, Amazon Customer Service.
Skills Needed: Communication, problem-solving, patience.
Examples: Technical support, order processing, account management.

5. Content Creation

5.1 Blogging

Description: Create and maintain a blog on topics of interest.
Platforms: WordPress, Blogger, Medium.
Monetization: Advertising (Google AdSense), affiliate marketing, sponsored posts.
Skills Needed: Writing, SEO, social media marketing.

Examples: Travel, lifestyle, personal finance, health and wellness.

5.2 YouTube Channel

Description: Produce and upload video content.
Monetization: Ad revenue, sponsorships, merchandise sales, memberships.
Skills Needed: Video production, editing, on-camera presence.
Examples: Tutorials, vlogs, reviews, educational content.

5.3 Podcasting

Description: Create and distribute audio content.
Monetization: Sponsorships, listener donations, merchandise sales.
Platforms: Anchor, Podbean, Spotify.
Skills Needed: Audio production, public speaking, marketing.
Examples: Interviews, storytelling, niche topics.

6. Investing and Trading

6.1 Stock Trading

Description: Buy and sell stocks for profit.
Platforms: Robinhood, E*TRADE, TD Ameritrade.
Skills Needed: Market analysis, risk management, financial knowledge.
Examples: Day trading, swing trading, long-term investing.

6.2 Real Estate Investing

Description: Invest in real estate through REITs or crowdfunding.
Platforms: Fundrise, RealtyMogul, Crowdstreet.
Skills Needed: Financial analysis, understanding of real estate markets.
Examples: Residential properties, commercial real estate, real estate funds.

6.3 Cryptocurrency

Description: Trade or invest in digital currencies.
Platforms: Coinbase, Binance, Kraken.
Skills Needed: Understanding of blockchain technology, market analysis.
Examples: Bitcoin, Ethereum, altcoins.

Practical Tips for Making Money from Home

Identify Your Skills and Interests: Choose opportunities that align with your strengths and passions.
Invest in Learning: Take courses or seek mentorship to enhance your skills.
Create a Dedicated Workspace: Set up a productive work environment at home.
Manage Time Effectively: Use tools like calendars and project management software to stay organized.
Market Your Services: Promote yourself through social media, networking, and online platforms.
Stay Updated: Keep abreast of trends and developments in your chosen field.
Balance Work and Life: Set boundaries to maintain a healthy work-life balance.

By exploring these avenues, you can find suitable ways to earn money from home, leveraging your skills and the power of the internet to achieve financial independence and flexibility.

Chapter 14: Overview of Work-from-Home Opportunities

In this chapter, we provide a comprehensive overview of various work-from-home opportunities. These opportunities range from freelance work and remote employment to running your own business and passive income generation. Each category offers distinct advantages and can be tailored to fit different skill sets and lifestyle preferences.

1. Freelancing
Freelancing allows you to offer your skills and services on a project-by-project basis. It provides flexibility and the ability to work with multiple clients.

1.1 Writing and Editing

Opportunities: Content writing, copywriting, proofreading, editing.
Platforms: Upwork, Fiverr, Freelancer, ProBlogger.
Skills Needed: Strong writing skills, attention to detail, ability to meet deadlines.
1.2 Graphic Design

Opportunities: Logo design, marketing materials, web design.
Platforms: 99designs, DesignCrowd, Dribbble, Behance.
Skills Needed: Proficiency in design software (Adobe Creative Suite), creativity, understanding of branding.

1.3 Web Development

Opportunities: Website creation, app development, website maintenance.
Platforms: Upwork, Toptal, GitHub Jobs.
Skills Needed: Coding languages (HTML, CSS, JavaScript), UX/UI design, problem-solving skills.

2. Remote Employment

Remote employment involves working for a company from your home. This can be a full-time or part-time arrangement and provides the stability of a regular paycheck.

2.1 Virtual Assistance

Opportunities: Administrative support, scheduling, email management.
Platforms: Belay, Time Etc, Zirtual.
Skills Needed: Organizational skills, communication, proficiency in office software.

2.2 Customer Service

Opportunities: Customer support, technical support, account management.
Platforms: LiveOps, Arise, Amazon Customer Service.
Skills Needed: Communication, problem-solving, patience.

2.3 Marketing and Social Media Management

Opportunities: Social media strategy, content creation, advertising management.
Platforms: Indeed, Remote.co, FlexJobs.
Skills Needed: Marketing knowledge, creativity, analytical skills.

3. Online Teaching and Tutoring

Teaching and tutoring online allow you to share your knowledge with students from around the world.

3.1 Online Courses

Opportunities: Course creation in various subjects.
Platforms: Udemy, Teachable, Coursera.
Skills Needed: Expertise in subject matter, ability to create engaging content.

3.2 Tutoring

Opportunities: Academic tutoring, test preparation, skill development.
Platforms: Chegg Tutors, Wyzant, Tutor.com.
Skills Needed: Proficiency in subject matter, communication skills, patience.

4. E-Commerce

Running an online store or selling products online provides the opportunity to earn money by leveraging the power of the internet.

4.1 Dropshipping

Opportunities: Selling products without holding inventory.
Platforms: Shopify, WooCommerce, Oberlo.
Skills Needed: Marketing, customer service, e-commerce platform knowledge.

4.2 Print on Demand

Opportunities: Selling custom-designed products like t-shirts, mugs, and phone cases.
Platforms: Printful, Printify, Redbubble, Teespring.
Skills Needed: Graphic design, marketing, e-commerce knowledge.

4.3 Handmade Goods

Opportunities: Selling handmade or customized products.
Platforms: Etsy, Handmade at Amazon, ArtFire.
Skills Needed: Craftsmanship, creativity, marketing.

5. Content Creation

Content creation allows you to monetize your creativity through various online platforms.

5.1 Blogging

Opportunities: Creating and maintaining a blog on topics of interest.
Platforms: WordPress, Blogger, Medium.
Monetization: Advertising, affiliate marketing, sponsored posts.
Skills Needed: Writing, SEO, social media marketing.

5.2 YouTube Channel

Opportunities: Producing and uploading video content.
Monetization: Ad revenue, sponsorships, merchandise sales, memberships.
Skills Needed: Video production, editing, on-camera presence.

5.3 Podcasting

Opportunities: Creating and distributing audio content.
Monetization: Sponsorships, listener donations, merchandise sales.
Platforms: Anchor, Podbean, Spotify.
Skills Needed: Audio production, public speaking, marketing.

6. Investing and Trading

Investing and trading provide opportunities to grow your wealth through financial markets.

6.1 Stock Trading

Opportunities: Buying and selling stocks for profit.
Platforms: Robinhood, E*TRADE, TD Ameritrade.
Skills Needed: Market analysis, risk management, financial knowledge.

6.2 Real Estate Investing

Opportunities: Investing in real estate through REITs or crowdfunding.
Platforms: Fundrise, RealtyMogul, Crowdstreet.
Skills Needed: Financial analysis, understanding of real estate markets.

6.3 Cryptocurrency

Opportunities: Trading or investing in digital currencies.
Platforms: Coinbase, Binance, Kraken.
Skills Needed: Understanding of blockchain technology, market analysis.

Choosing the Right Work-from-Home Opportunity
To select the best work-from-home opportunity for you, consider the following factors:

Skills and Interests: Choose opportunities that align with your skills and passions.
Time Commitment: Consider the amount of time you can dedicate to the work.
Income Potential: Evaluate the earning potential and whether it meets your financial goals.
Flexibility: Determine how much flexibility you need in your work schedule.
Initial Investment: Assess any upfront costs required to start the opportunity.
Long-Term Viability: Consider whether the opportunity is sustainable and can grow over time.

Practical Tips for Success
Create a Dedicated Workspace: Set up a comfortable and productive work environment at home.
Set a Schedule: Establish a routine to manage your time effectively.
Stay Organized: Use tools like calendars, to-do lists, and project management software to stay on track.

Invest in Learning: Continuously improve your skills and stay updated on industry trends.

Network and Market Yourself: Build a network of contacts and promote your services or products.

Maintain Work-Life Balance: Set boundaries to ensure a healthy balance between work and personal life.

By exploring and leveraging these work-from-home opportunities, you can find suitable ways to earn money, achieve financial independence, and enjoy the flexibility of working from home.

Chapter 15: Setting Up a Productive Home Office

Creating a productive home office is crucial for maintaining focus, efficiency, and work-life balance when working from home. This chapter will guide you through the essential steps and considerations for setting up a home office that maximizes your productivity and comfort.

1. Choosing the Right Location
1.1 Evaluate Space Availability

Dedicated Room: If possible, choose a separate room to serve as your home office to minimize distractions and establish clear boundaries between work and personal life.
Corner of a Room: If a dedicated room isn't available, select a quiet corner of a room with minimal foot traffic and distractions.
1.2 Consider Lighting

Natural Light: Position your desk near a window to take advantage of natural light, which can improve mood and productivity.
Artificial Lighting: Ensure adequate artificial lighting, including a combination of ambient, task, and accent lighting to reduce eye strain and create a comfortable work environment.

1.3 Noise Levels

Quiet Area: Choose a location away from high-traffic areas and noisy appliances.
Soundproofing: Consider adding soundproofing elements like thick carpets, curtains, or acoustic panels if noise is an issue.

2. Essential Furniture and Equipment

2.1 Ergonomic Desk and Chair

Desk: Select a desk with ample surface area to accommodate your computer, documents, and other essentials. Adjustable desks that allow for both sitting and standing positions are ideal.
Chair: Invest in an ergonomic chair that provides proper lumbar support, adjustable height, and comfortable cushioning.

2.2 Computer and Accessories

Computer: Choose a reliable computer that meets the demands of your work, whether it's a desktop or laptop.
Monitor: Use an external monitor to reduce eye strain and improve posture. Position it at eye level, about an arm's length away.
Keyboard and Mouse: Opt for an ergonomic keyboard and mouse to reduce strain on your hands and wrists.

2.3 Internet and Connectivity

High-Speed Internet: Ensure you have a fast and reliable internet connection to support video calls, file uploads/downloads, and other online activities.
Router Placement: Position your router close to your workspace or use a Wi-Fi extender to ensure a strong signal.

2.4 Office Supplies and Storage

Supplies: Stock up on essential office supplies such as pens, notepads, sticky notes, and a printer.

Storage: Use shelves, filing cabinets, or storage boxes to organize documents and office supplies, keeping your workspace clutter-free.

3. Organizing Your Workspace

3.1 Desk Organization

Declutter: Keep your desk free of unnecessary items. Only keep essential items within reach.

Organizers: Use desk organizers, trays, and cable management solutions to maintain order and reduce clutter.

3.2 Filing System

Digital Files: Organize digital files using a logical folder structure. Consider cloud storage solutions like Google Drive, Dropbox, or OneDrive for easy access and backup.

Physical Files: Use labeled folders and filing cabinets for physical documents. Implement a regular filing routine to keep everything in order.

3.3 Productivity Tools

Task Management: Utilize task management tools like Trello, Asana, or Todoist to track projects and deadlines.

Calendars: Keep a physical or digital calendar to schedule appointments, meetings, and deadlines.

Timers and Clocks: Use timers to implement techniques like the Pomodoro Technique, which can help you manage your time and maintain focus.

4. Enhancing Comfort and Well-Being

4.1 Ergonomics

Posture: Maintain a proper sitting posture with your feet flat on the ground, elbows at a 90-degree angle, and your back supported.

Breaks: Take regular breaks to stand, stretch, and move around to prevent stiffness and fatigue.

4.2 Personalization

Decor: Personalize your workspace with items that inspire and motivate you, such as photos, plants, or artwork.
Comfort Items: Include comfort items like a cozy blanket, cushion, or footrest to make your workspace more inviting.

4.3 Health Considerations

Air Quality: Ensure good air quality by keeping your workspace well-ventilated and using air purifiers if necessary.
Hydration and Snacks: Keep a water bottle and healthy snacks at your desk to stay hydrated and maintain energy levels.

5. Establishing a Routine

5.1 Set Work Hours

Consistent Schedule: Establish regular work hours and stick to them to create a sense of normalcy and routine.
Boundaries: Clearly communicate your work hours to family members or housemates to minimize interruptions.

5.2 Morning Routine

Start Your Day Right: Begin your day with a morning routine that prepares you mentally and physically for work, such as exercise, meditation, or a healthy breakfast.

5.3 End-of-Day Routine

Wind Down: Create an end-of-day routine to signal the end of the workday, such as tidying your desk, making a to-do list for the next day, or engaging in a relaxing activity.

6. Maintaining Work-Life Balance

6.1 Separate Work and Personal Life

Physical Separation: Use your home office only for work to create a physical separation between work and personal life.
Mental Separation: Develop habits that help you transition between work mode and personal time, such as changing clothes after work or taking a walk.

6.2 Set Boundaries

Work Hours: Stick to your designated work hours and avoid working late unless absolutely necessary.
Breaks: Take regular breaks throughout the day to rest and recharge. Use these breaks to engage in activities unrelated to work.

6.3 Self-Care

Exercise: Incorporate physical activity into your daily routine to boost your energy and reduce stress.
Mental Health: Practice mindfulness, meditation, or other relaxation techniques to maintain your mental well-being.
By following these guidelines, you can create a home office that enhances your productivity, comfort, and overall well-being. A well-designed workspace is essential for maintaining focus and achieving success while working from home.

Chapter 16: Balancing Work and Home Life

Balancing work and home life is essential for maintaining productivity, well-being, and a healthy personal life when working from home. This chapter provides strategies and tips to help you effectively manage your professional responsibilities while enjoying your personal time.

1. Establish Clear Boundaries
1.1 Define Your Work Hours

Consistent Schedule: Set specific work hours and stick to them. This helps create a clear division between work time and personal time.
Communicate Boundaries: Inform family members, housemates, or anyone else you live with about your work schedule to minimize interruptions.
1.2 Physical Boundaries

Dedicated Workspace: Use a specific area in your home solely for work. This helps mentally separate work from personal life.
Leave Work Behind: At the end of your workday, leave your designated workspace to signal that work is over.
2. Create a Routine

2.1 Morning Routine

Start Your Day Right: Establish a morning routine that prepares you for the day ahead, such as exercising, having a healthy breakfast, or meditating.
Dress for Success: Dressing in work-appropriate clothes, even when working from home, can help you get into a professional mindset.

2.2 End-of-Day Routine

Wind Down: Develop an end-of-day routine to transition from work mode to personal time. This could include tidying your workspace, planning for the next day, or engaging in a relaxing activity.

3. Manage Your Time Effectively

3.1 Prioritize Tasks

To-Do Lists: Create daily to-do lists to prioritize your tasks. Focus on completing the most important tasks first.
Time Blocks: Use time-blocking techniques to allocate specific periods for different tasks, ensuring a balanced workload.

3.2 Avoid Multitasking

Focus on One Task: Concentrate on one task at a time to improve efficiency and reduce stress.
Minimize Distractions: Identify common distractions and find ways to minimize them, such as using noise-cancelling headphones or setting specific times for checking emails.

4. Take Regular Breaks

4.1 Short Breaks

Pomodoro Technique: Use techniques like the Pomodoro Technique, which involves working for 25 minutes and then taking a 5-minute break. This helps maintain focus and prevent burnout.

Movement Breaks: Take short breaks to stand, stretch, and move around to keep your body active and reduce the risk of fatigue.

4.2 Longer Breaks

Lunch Break: Take a longer break for lunch to recharge and avoid eating at your desk.

Scheduled Time Off: Plan regular days off to rest and engage in activities you enjoy.

5. Leverage Technology

5.1 Productivity Tools

Task Management: Use task management tools like Trello, Asana, or Todoist to organize tasks and deadlines.

Calendars: Keep a digital calendar to schedule work tasks, meetings, and personal activities.

5.2 Communication Tools

Set Expectations: Use communication tools like Slack or Microsoft Teams to stay in touch with colleagues and set expectations for availability.

Limit Notifications: Manage your notification settings to reduce interruptions during focused work periods.

6. Maintain Health and Well-Being

6.1 Physical Health

Exercise: Incorporate regular physical activity into your daily routine. Exercise helps reduce stress, boost energy levels, and improve overall health.

Ergonomics: Ensure your workspace is ergonomically designed to prevent physical strain. Use a comfortable chair, proper desk height, and monitor placement.

6.2 Mental Health

Mindfulness: Practice mindfulness or meditation to reduce stress and increase focus. Apps like Headspace or Calm can be helpful.

Support Network: Stay connected with friends and family for emotional support. Regularly communicate with loved ones to maintain strong relationships.

7. Set Realistic Expectations

7.1 Manage Workload

Set Limits: Be realistic about what you can accomplish in a day. Avoid overcommitting to tasks and learn to say no when necessary.

Delegate: If possible, delegate tasks to others to manage your workload effectively.

7.2 Be Flexible

Adapt to Changes: Be prepared to adjust your schedule and priorities as needed. Flexibility is key to maintaining balance.

Accept Imperfections: Understand that not every day will be perfectly balanced. Accept occasional disruptions and focus on getting back on track.

8. Engage in Personal Activities

8.1 Hobbies and Interests

Pursue Hobbies: Dedicate time to hobbies and interests outside of work to relax and recharge.

Learn New Skills: Consider learning new skills or taking up new hobbies to keep your mind engaged and balanced.

8.2 Quality Family Time

Family Activities: Plan activities with family members, such as game nights, movie nights, or outdoor outings.

Unplug: Spend quality time with loved ones without the distraction of electronic devices.

Practical Tips for Success

Set Clear Goals: Define what work-life balance means to you and set clear goals to achieve it.
Regular Reflection: Periodically review your work-life balance and make adjustments as needed.
Seek Support: If you're struggling to balance work and home life, seek advice or support from friends, family, or a professional.
Prioritize Self-Care: Make self-care a priority by ensuring you have time for relaxation, hobbies, and activities that bring you joy.
Stay Organized: Keep your work and personal life organized with schedules, to-do lists, and a tidy workspace.
By implementing these strategies, you can create a balanced and fulfilling work-from-home lifestyle that supports both your professional and personal well-being.

Chapter 17: Investing for Financial Growth

Investing is a powerful tool for building wealth and achieving financial goals over the long term. In this chapter, we'll explore the fundamentals of investing, different investment options, and strategies for successful investing to help you grow your wealth.

1. Understanding the Basics of Investing
1.1 What is Investing?

Definition: Investing involves committing money to an asset with the expectation of earning a return or profit in the future. Purpose: Investing allows you to grow your wealth, beat inflation, and achieve financial goals such as retirement, education, or buying a home.
1.2 Key Investment Principles

Risk and Return: Generally, higher returns are associated with higher risk. Understanding your risk tolerance is essential for building a diversified investment portfolio.

Time Horizon: The longer your investment horizon, the more risk you can afford to take, as you have more time to ride out market fluctuations.

Diversification: Spreading your investments across different asset classes helps reduce risk and optimize returns.

2. Investment Options

2.1 Stocks

Definition: Stocks represent ownership in a company. Investing in stocks offers the potential for high returns but comes with higher volatility and risk.

Types: Common stocks, preferred stocks, growth stocks, value stocks, dividend stocks.

Platforms: Online brokerage accounts, robo-advisors, mutual funds, exchange-traded funds (ETFs).

2.2 Bonds

Definition: Bonds are debt securities issued by governments, corporations, or municipalities. Investing in bonds provides income through regular interest payments and return of principal at maturity.

Types: Government bonds, corporate bonds, municipal bonds, Treasury bonds.

Platforms: Brokerage accounts, bond funds, bond ETFs.

2.3 Real Estate

Definition: Real estate investing involves purchasing properties or real estate investment trusts (REITs) to generate rental income or capital appreciation.

Types: Residential properties, commercial properties, REITs, real estate crowdfunding.

Platforms: Real estate platforms, crowdfunding platforms, real estate investment apps.

2.4 Mutual Funds and ETFs

Definition: Mutual funds and ETFs pool money from multiple investors to invest in a diversified portfolio of stocks, bonds, or other assets.
Benefits: Provides instant diversification, professional management, and liquidity.
Platforms: Online brokerage accounts, mutual fund companies, ETF providers.

2.5 Retirement Accounts

Definition: Retirement accounts like 401(k)s, IRAs, and Roth IRAs offer tax advantages for long-term investing.
Benefits: Tax-deferred or tax-free growth, employer matching contributions, flexibility in investment options.
Platforms: Employer-sponsored retirement plans, brokerage firms, banks.

3. Strategies for Successful Investing

3.1 Set Clear Goals

Short-Term vs. Long-Term Goals: Define your investment objectives, whether it's saving for retirement, buying a house, or funding education.
Risk Tolerance: Assess your risk tolerance and investment horizon to determine an appropriate asset allocation.

3.2 Diversify Your Portfolio

Asset Allocation: Allocate your investments across different asset classes (stocks, bonds, real estate) based on your risk tolerance and investment goals.
Rebalance Regularly: Periodically review and rebalance your portfolio to maintain your target asset allocation.

3.3 Invest Consistently

Dollar-Cost Averaging: Invest a fixed amount of money regularly, regardless of market fluctuations. This strategy helps reduce the impact of market volatility over time.
Automatic Investing: Set up automatic contributions to your investment accounts to ensure consistency and discipline.

3.4 Stay Informed

Continuous Learning: Stay informed about market trends, economic indicators, and investment strategies through books, articles, and reputable financial news sources.
Seek Professional Advice: Consider consulting with a financial advisor or investment professional for personalized guidance and advice.

4. Risk Management

4.1 Understand Risk

Types of Risk: Market risk, inflation risk, interest rate risk, credit risk, liquidity risk.
Diversification: Diversify your investments across different asset classes and sectors to mitigate specific risks.

4.2 Emergency Fund

Importance: Maintain an emergency fund with enough cash to cover 3-6 months of living expenses. This fund acts as a buffer during financial emergencies and allows you to avoid tapping into your investments prematurely.

5. Monitor and Adjust Your Portfolio

5.1 Regular Review

Monitor Performance: Periodically review the performance of your investments and assess whether they align with your goals and risk tolerance.
Adjust Allocation: Make adjustments to your portfolio allocation as needed based on changes in your financial situation, market conditions, or investment objectives.

5.2 Tax Considerations

Tax-Efficient Investing: Utilize tax-efficient investment strategies, such as holding investments in tax-advantaged accounts and minimizing portfolio turnover to reduce tax liabilities.

Tax-Loss Harvesting: Offset capital gains with capital losses by selling losing investments to reduce tax obligations.

6. Long-Term Perspective

6.1 Patience

Stay the Course: Avoid making impulsive investment decisions based on short-term market fluctuations. Focus on your long-term investment objectives and stay disciplined.

Power of Compounding: Harness the power of compounding by reinvesting dividends and letting your investments grow over time.

6.2 Review and Adjust

Adapt to Changes: Be flexible and adaptable in your investment approach. Review and adjust your strategy as necessary to reflect changes in your financial goals, risk tolerance, and market conditions.

Conclusion

Investing for financial growth requires patience, discipline, and a long-term perspective. By understanding the basics of investing, diversifying your portfolio, and adhering to sound investment principles, you can build wealth and achieve your financial goals over time. Remember to stay informed, regularly monitor your investments, and seek professional advice when needed. With careful planning and consistent effort, you can pave the way for a secure financial future.

Chapter 18: Investing for Beginners

Investing can seem daunting for beginners, but it's an essential step toward building wealth and achieving financial goals. In this chapter, we'll provide a beginner-friendly guide to investing, covering the basics, investment options, and tips to get started on your investment journey.

1. Understanding the Basics
1.1 What is Investing?

Investing involves putting money into assets with the expectation of generating income or profit over time.
The goal of investing is to grow your wealth and achieve financial objectives, such as retirement savings, purchasing a home, or funding education.

1.2 Risk and Return

Investments come with varying levels of risk and potential return. Generally, higher returns are associated with higher risk.

Understanding your risk tolerance is crucial for determining an appropriate investment strategy.

1.3 Time Horizon

Your investment time horizon refers to the length of time you plan to hold your investments before needing to access the funds.

Longer time horizons allow you to take on more risk and potentially benefit from the power of compounding.

2. Investment Options for Beginners

2.1 Stocks

Stocks represent ownership in a company. Investing in stocks can offer high returns but comes with higher volatility. Beginners can start with index funds or exchange-traded funds (ETFs) to gain exposure to a diversified portfolio of stocks.

2.2 Bonds

Bonds are debt securities issued by governments, corporations, or municipalities. They provide regular interest payments and return of principal at maturity.

Beginners may consider investing in bond funds or Treasury securities for a more conservative investment option.

2.3 Mutual Funds and ETFs

Mutual funds and ETFs pool money from multiple investors to invest in a diversified portfolio of stocks, bonds, or other assets.

These investment vehicles offer instant diversification and are suitable for beginners looking for a hands-off approach to investing.

2.4 Retirement Accounts

Retirement accounts like 401(k)s and IRAs offer tax advantages for long-term investing. Many employers offer employer-sponsored retirement plans with matching contributions.

Beginners should take advantage of employer matching contributions and consider investing in low-cost index funds or target-date funds within their retirement accounts.

3. Tips for Getting Started

3.1 Set Clear Goals

Define your investment objectives and establish clear financial goals. Determine your risk tolerance and investment time horizon.

3.2 Educate Yourself

Take the time to educate yourself about investing. Read books, articles, and reputable financial websites to understand basic investment principles and strategies.

3.3 Start Small

Begin with small, manageable investments, especially if you're new to investing. Consider starting with low-cost index funds or ETFs to build your investment portfolio gradually.

3.4 Diversify Your Portfolio

Diversification is key to reducing risk in your investment portfolio. Spread your investments across different asset classes, industries, and geographic regions.

3.5 Invest Regularly

Consistent investing, even with small amounts, can lead to significant long-term growth. Set up automatic contributions to your investment accounts to maintain discipline.

3.6 Stay Disciplined

Avoid making impulsive investment decisions based on short-term market fluctuations. Stick to your investment plan and resist the temptation to time the market.

4. Monitor and Review Your Investments

4.1 Regularly Review Your Portfolio

Periodically review your investment portfolio to ensure it remains aligned with your financial goals and risk tolerance. Rebalance your portfolio as needed to maintain your target asset allocation.

4.2 Stay Informed

Stay informed about market trends, economic indicators, and investment news. Keep up with changes in your investment portfolio and adjust your strategy accordingly.

4.3 Seek Professional Advice

Consider consulting with a financial advisor or investment professional, especially as your investment portfolio grows. A professional can provide personalized guidance and help you navigate complex investment decisions.

Conclusion

Investing for beginners is an important step toward financial independence and long-term wealth building. By understanding the basics of investing, choosing suitable investment options, and following a disciplined approach, beginners can set themselves on the path to financial success. Remember to start small, stay informed, and remain patient as you embark on your investment journey. With time, dedication, and smart decision-making, you can achieve your financial goals and secure a brighter financial future.

Chapter 19: Basic Principles of Investing

Understanding the fundamental principles of investing is essential for making informed decisions and building a successful investment portfolio. In this chapter, we'll explore the basic principles that guide investment strategies and help investors achieve their financial goals.

1. Start Early and Invest Regularly
1.1 The Power of Compounding

Compounding allows your investment returns to generate additional returns over time.
Starting to invest early and consistently contributing to your investments can significantly increase your wealth over the long term.

1.2 Dollar-Cost Averaging

Dollar-cost averaging involves investing a fixed amount of money at regular intervals, regardless of market fluctuations. This strategy helps smooth out market volatility and can result in lower average purchase prices over time.

2. Set Clear Investment Goals

2.1 Define Your Objectives

Clearly define your investment goals, whether it's saving for retirement, buying a home, or funding education.
Your investment goals will guide your asset allocation, risk tolerance, and investment strategy.

2.2 Consider Time Horizon

Your investment time horizon refers to the length of time you plan to hold your investments before needing to access the funds.
Longer time horizons allow you to take on more risk and potentially benefit from higher returns.

3. Diversify Your Portfolio

3.1 Spread Your Risk

Diversification involves spreading your investments across different asset classes, industries, and geographic regions. Diversifying your portfolio helps reduce the impact of any single investment's performance on your overall portfolio.

3.2 Asset Allocation

Asset allocation refers to the distribution of your investments among different asset classes such as stocks, bonds, and cash equivalents.
Your asset allocation should be based on your investment goals, risk tolerance, and time horizon.

4. Understand Risk and Reward

4.1 Risk Tolerance

Risk tolerance refers to your ability and willingness to withstand fluctuations in the value of your investments. Understanding your risk tolerance is crucial for determining an appropriate investment strategy and asset allocation.

4.2 Relationship Between Risk and Reward

Generally, investments with higher potential returns come with higher levels of risk.
Balancing risk and reward is essential for building a diversified investment portfolio that aligns with your financial goals.

5. Invest in What You Understand

5.1 Knowledge is Key

Invest in assets and investment products that you understand and feel comfortable with.
Avoid investing in complex financial instruments or products that you don't fully comprehend.

5.2 Do Your Research

Conduct thorough research before making investment decisions. Understand the fundamentals of the companies or assets you're investing in and evaluate their growth prospects, financial health, and competitive position.

6. Stay Disciplined and Patient

6.1 Avoid Emotional Investing

Emotional investing, such as buying or selling investments based on fear or greed, can lead to poor decision-making and underperformance.
Stick to your investment plan and avoid making impulsive decisions during periods of market volatility.

6.2 Long-Term Perspective

Investing is a long-term endeavor, and short-term fluctuations are normal.
Stay focused on your investment goals and remain patient, even during periods of market uncertainty.

7. Monitor and Rebalance Your Portfolio

7.1 Regular Review

Periodically review your investment portfolio to ensure it remains aligned with your investment goals and risk tolerance.
Rebalance your portfolio as needed to maintain your target asset allocation and risk level.

7.2 Stay Informed

Stay informed about market trends, economic indicators, and changes in your investment portfolio.
Keep up with financial news and developments that may impact your investments.

8. Seek Professional Advice When Needed

8.1 Financial Advisor

Consider consulting with a financial advisor or investment professional, especially for complex investment decisions or financial planning.
A professional can provide personalized guidance, help you navigate market fluctuations, and ensure your investment strategy aligns with your goals.

8.2 Continuous Learning

Invest in your financial education and continuously seek to improve your knowledge and understanding of investing. Take advantage of resources such as books, online courses, and seminars to expand your investment expertise.

Conclusion

By following these basic principles of investing, you can build a solid foundation for achieving your financial goals and building long-term wealth. Remember to start early, diversify your portfolio, and stay disciplined and patient throughout your investment journey. With careful planning, informed decision-making, and a long-term perspective, you can create a successful investment strategy that helps you secure your financial future.

Chapter 20: Types of Investments: Stocks, Bonds, Mutual Funds

Investors have a wide array of investment options to choose from, each with its own characteristics, risks, and potential returns. In this chapter, we'll explore three common types of investments: stocks, bonds, and mutual funds, providing an overview of each and discussing their key features.

1. Stocks
1.1 Definition

Stocks, also known as equities, represent ownership in a company. When you buy stocks, you become a shareholder and own a portion of the company's assets and earnings. Stockholders may benefit from capital appreciation if the company's value increases, as well as dividends if the company distributes profits to shareholders.
1.2 Key Features

Risk and Return: Stocks offer the potential for high returns but come with higher volatility and risk compared to other investments.
Types: Common stocks, preferred stocks, growth stocks, value stocks, dividend stocks.
Platforms: Stocks can be bought and sold through online brokerage accounts, traditional brokerage firms, and investment apps.
2. Bonds
2.1 Definition

Bonds are debt securities issued by governments, corporations, or municipalities to raise capital. When you buy a bond, you are essentially lending money to the issuer in exchange for regular interest payments and repayment of the principal amount at maturity.
Bonds are typically considered lower-risk investments compared to stocks and offer fixed income streams.

2.2 Key Features

Risk and Return: Bonds generally offer lower returns than stocks but come with lower risk and volatility. The level of risk depends on the creditworthiness of the issuer.
Types: Government bonds, corporate bonds, municipal bonds, Treasury bonds.
Platforms: Bonds can be purchased through brokerage accounts, bond mutual funds, bond ETFs, and directly from issuers in the case of Treasury securities.

3. Mutual Funds

3.1 Definition

Mutual funds are investment vehicles that pool money from multiple investors to invest in a diversified portfolio of stocks, bonds, or other assets. They are managed by professional fund managers, who make investment decisions on behalf of investors.
Mutual funds offer instant diversification and are suitable for investors who prefer a hands-off approach to investing.

3.2 Key Features

Diversification: Mutual funds invest in a variety of securities, allowing investors to spread their risk across different assets and sectors.
Professional Management: Fund managers oversee the investment decisions and portfolio management, aiming to achieve the fund's investment objectives.

Types: Equity funds, bond funds, balanced funds, index funds, target-date funds.

Platforms: Mutual funds are available through brokerage firms, financial institutions, and retirement accounts.

4. Choosing the Right Investment

4.1 Consider Your Goals and Risk Tolerance

When selecting investments, consider your investment goals, risk tolerance, and time horizon. Stocks may be suitable for long-term growth, while bonds offer stability and income. Diversification across asset classes can help manage risk and optimize returns.

4.2 Evaluate Investment Options

Research and evaluate investment options based on factors such as historical performance, fees, and investment strategy. Consider consulting with a financial advisor or investment professional to help you select investments that align with your goals and risk tolerance.

5. Monitoring and Rebalancing

5.1 Regular Review

Periodically review your investment portfolio to ensure it remains aligned with your investment goals and risk tolerance.

Monitor the performance of your investments and make adjustments as needed based on changes in your financial situation or market conditions.

5.2 Rebalancing

Rebalance your portfolio as needed to maintain your target asset allocation. Selling investments that have become overweighted and reinvesting the proceeds in underweighted assets can help keep your portfolio aligned with your goals.

6. Risks Associated with Investments

6.1 Market Risk

Market risk refers to the possibility of investments losing value due to factors such as economic downturns, market volatility, or geopolitical events.
Diversification and a long-term investment horizon can help mitigate market risk.

6.2 Credit Risk

Credit risk is the risk that bond issuers may default on their debt obligations, leading to loss of principal or missed interest payments.
Investing in bonds with higher credit ratings can help reduce credit risk.

Conclusion

Stocks, bonds, and mutual funds are foundational investment options that offer investors opportunities for growth, income, and diversification. By understanding the characteristics and risks associated with each type of investment, investors can build well-rounded portfolios that align with their financial goals and risk tolerance. Remember to regularly monitor your investments, stay informed about market developments, and seek professional advice when needed to make informed investment decisions.

Chapter 21: Understanding Risk and Return

Risk and return are two fundamental concepts in investing that are inherently linked. Investors must understand the relationship between risk and return to make informed investment decisions and build portfolios that align with their financial goals and risk tolerance. In this chapter, we'll explore the concepts of risk and return, their relationship, and strategies for managing investment risk effectively.

1. What is Risk?
1.1 Definition

Risk refers to the uncertainty or variability of investment returns. It encompasses the possibility of losing some or all of the investment principal or receiving lower-than-expected returns.
Different types of risk include market risk, credit risk, inflation risk, interest rate risk, and liquidity risk.
1.2 Types of Investment Risk

Market Risk: The risk of investments losing value due to factors such as economic conditions, market volatility, or geopolitical events.
Credit Risk: The risk that bond issuers may default on their debt obligations, resulting in loss of principal or missed interest payments.
Inflation Risk: The risk that inflation will erode the purchasing power of investment returns over time.
Interest Rate Risk: The risk that changes in interest rates will affect the value of fixed-income investments, such as bonds.

Liquidity Risk: The risk that investments cannot be easily converted into cash without significant loss of value.

2. What is Return?

2.1 Definition

Return refers to the gain or loss generated on an investment over a specific period, expressed as a percentage of the investment's initial value.

Returns can come from capital appreciation, dividends, interest payments, or other sources.

2.2 Types of Investment Return

Capital Gains: The increase in the value of an investment over time. Capital gains are realized when an investment is sold for a higher price than its purchase price.

Dividend Income: Payments made by companies to their shareholders from profits. Dividends can provide a steady stream of income for investors.

Interest Income: Income earned from fixed-income investments, such as bonds or certificates of deposit (CDs).

Total Return: The overall return on an investment, including both capital appreciation and income.

3. Relationship Between Risk and Return

3.1 Risk-Return Tradeoff

The risk-return tradeoff is the principle that higher levels of risk are generally associated with higher potential returns, and vice versa.

Investors must weigh the potential for higher returns against the increased risk of loss when making investment decisions.

3.2 Assessing Risk Tolerance

Risk tolerance refers to an investor's ability and willingness to withstand fluctuations in the value of their investments. Understanding your risk tolerance is crucial for determining an appropriate investment strategy and asset allocation.

4. Strategies for Managing Risk
4.1 Diversification

Diversification involves spreading investments across different asset classes, industries, and geographic regions to reduce the impact of any single investment's performance on the overall portfolio.

Diversification can help manage risk and optimize returns by ensuring that not all investments are affected by the same market conditions.

4.2 Asset Allocation

Asset allocation refers to the distribution of investments among different asset classes, such as stocks, bonds, and cash equivalents.

A well-balanced asset allocation strategy can help manage risk by aligning investments with your investment goals, time horizon, and risk tolerance.

4.3 Regular Monitoring and Rebalancing

Periodically review your investment portfolio to ensure it remains aligned with your investment goals and risk tolerance.

Rebalance your portfolio as needed to maintain your target asset allocation, especially after significant market movements or changes in your financial situation.

5. Conclusion

Understanding the concepts of risk and return is essential for making informed investment decisions and building portfolios that align with your financial goals and risk tolerance. By recognizing the risk-return tradeoff and implementing strategies to manage risk effectively, investors can achieve a balance between maximizing returns and protecting their investments from adverse market conditions. Remember to regularly monitor your investments, stay informed about market developments, and seek professional advice when needed to navigate the complex landscape of investment risk and return.

Chapter 22: Stock Market Investing

Investing in the stock market can be a rewarding way to build wealth over the long term, but it also comes with risks and complexities. In this chapter, we'll explore how the stock market works, strategies for stock market investing, and common mistakes to avoid.

1. How the Stock Market Works
1.1 Definition

The stock market is a marketplace where investors buy and sell shares of publicly traded companies. It provides a platform for companies to raise capital by issuing stocks and for investors to invest in those stocks.
1.2 Participants

Companies: Companies issue stocks to raise capital for growth, expansion, or other business activities.

Investors: Individuals, institutional investors, and fund managers buy and sell stocks to build investment portfolios and generate returns.

Exchanges: Stock exchanges, such as the New York Stock Exchange (NYSE) and Nasdaq, facilitate the trading of stocks by providing a centralized marketplace.

1.3 Price Determination

Stock prices are determined by supply and demand dynamics in the market. When there is high demand for a stock, its price tends to rise, and vice versa.

Factors such as company performance, economic conditions, investor sentiment, and geopolitical events influence stock prices.

2. Strategies for Stock Market Investing

2.1 Fundamental Analysis

Fundamental analysis involves evaluating a company's financial health, business prospects, management team, and competitive position to determine its intrinsic value.

Investors use financial statements, earnings reports, industry trends, and other data to assess the value of a company's stock.

2.2 Technical Analysis

Technical analysis involves analyzing historical price and volume data to identify patterns and trends in stock prices. Technical analysts use charts, indicators, and statistical tools to make investment decisions based on past price movements.

2.3 Buy and Hold Strategy

The buy and hold strategy involves buying high-quality stocks and holding them for the long term, regardless of short-term market fluctuations.

This strategy is based on the belief that the stock market tends to trend upward over time, and holding quality stocks can generate significant returns over the long term.

2.4 Dollar-Cost Averaging

Dollar-cost averaging involves investing a fixed amount of money at regular intervals, regardless of market conditions. This strategy helps smooth out market volatility and can result in lower average purchase prices over time.

3. Common Mistakes to Avoid

3.1 Emotional Investing

Making investment decisions based on emotions, such as fear or greed, can lead to poor outcomes. It's essential to stay disciplined and stick to your investment plan, even during periods of market volatility.

3.2 Overtrading

Overtrading, or excessive buying and selling of stocks, can lead to high transaction costs, taxes, and reduced investment returns. It's important to avoid frequent trading and focus on long-term investing goals.

3.3 Lack of Diversification

Failing to diversify your investment portfolio can expose you to unnecessary risk. Investing in a variety of asset classes, industries, and geographic regions can help mitigate risk and optimize returns.

3.4 Ignoring Fundamentals

Ignoring fundamental analysis and blindly following stock tips or market trends can lead to poor investment decisions. It's crucial to conduct thorough research and analysis before investing in any stock.

3.5 Timing the Market

Trying to time the market by predicting short-term price movements is difficult and risky. Instead of trying to buy stocks at the lowest prices and sell at the highest prices, focus on long-term investment fundamentals and stay invested through market cycles.

4. Conclusion

Investing in the stock market can be a rewarding way to build wealth over time, but it requires careful planning, research, and discipline. By understanding how the stock market works, employing sound investment strategies, and avoiding common pitfalls, investors can increase their chances of success and achieve their financial goals. Remember to stay informed, stay disciplined, and seek professional advice when needed to navigate the complexities of stock market investing.

Chapter 23: Personal Finance Management

Personal finance management is crucial for achieving financial stability, security, and independence. In this chapter, we'll explore the importance of personal finance, discuss budgeting and expense tracking strategies, and highlight the significance of building an emergency fund.

1. Importance of Personal Finance
1.1 Financial Stability

Effective personal finance management helps individuals maintain financial stability by ensuring they can cover essential expenses, save for the future, and weather unexpected financial challenges.

1.2 Financial Security

Personal finance management plays a key role in achieving financial security, allowing individuals to build savings, reduce debt, and prepare for long-term financial goals such as retirement or homeownership.

1.3 Financial Independence

By managing their finances wisely, individuals can work towards financial independence, where they have the resources and freedom to live life on their own terms without relying on others for financial support.

2. Budgeting and Expense Tracking

2.1 Budgeting Basics

Budgeting involves creating a plan for how you will allocate your income to cover expenses, save for goals, and pay off debt.

Start by tracking your income and expenses to understand where your money is going and identify areas for improvement.

2.2 Creating a Budget

List all sources of income and categorize expenses into fixed (e.g., rent, utilities) and variable (e.g., groceries, entertainment).

Allocate a portion of your income to savings and debt repayment, and prioritize essential expenses while minimizing discretionary spending.

2.3 Expense Tracking

Use tools such as budgeting apps, spreadsheets, or pen and paper to track your expenses regularly.

Review your spending habits, identify unnecessary expenses, and make adjustments to align your spending with your financial goals.

3. Building an Emergency Fund

3.1 Importance of an Emergency Fund

An emergency fund is a financial cushion that provides peace of mind and protection against unexpected expenses or financial emergencies.

Having an emergency fund helps individuals avoid relying on credit cards or loans to cover unexpected costs and reduces the risk of financial hardship.

3.2 How Much to Save

Aim to save enough to cover 3-6 months' worth of living expenses in your emergency fund.

Consider factors such as your income stability, job security, and potential expenses (e.g., medical bills, car repairs) when determining the appropriate size of your emergency fund.

3.3 Building Your Emergency Fund

Start by setting a savings goal and establishing a separate savings account specifically for your emergency fund.

Contribute to your emergency fund regularly, even if it's just a small amount each month, and avoid dipping into it for non-emergency purposes.

4. Conclusion

Personal finance management is essential for achieving financial well-being and peace of mind. By creating and following a budget, tracking expenses, and building an emergency fund, individuals can take control of their finances, reduce financial stress, and work towards their long-term financial goals. Remember to regularly review and adjust your financial plan as needed, stay disciplined in your spending and saving habits, and seek professional advice when necessary to ensure financial success.

Chapter 24: Specialized Investment Strategies

In addition to traditional investment approaches, specialized investment strategies offer unique opportunities for investors to achieve their financial goals and tailor their portfolios to specific objectives or market conditions. In this chapter, we'll explore some specialized investment strategies, their features, and considerations for implementing them effectively.

1. Value Investing
1.1 Definition

Value investing involves selecting stocks that are trading at a discount to their intrinsic value based on fundamental analysis.

Value investors seek to buy undervalued stocks with the potential for long-term capital appreciation as the market recognizes their true worth.

1.2 Key Features

Focus on companies with strong fundamentals, such as low price-to-earnings (P/E) ratios, high dividend yields, and solid balance sheets.

Patience is essential, as value stocks may take time to be recognized by the market.

2. Growth Investing

2.1 Definition

Growth investing focuses on identifying companies with strong growth potential in terms of earnings, revenue, or market share.

Growth investors are willing to pay higher prices for stocks with the expectation of above-average future returns.

2.2 Key Features

Emphasis on companies with innovative products or services, expanding markets, and sustainable competitive advantages.

Growth stocks may be more volatile than value stocks but offer the potential for significant capital appreciation over time.

3. Dividend Investing

3.1 Definition

Dividend investing involves selecting stocks that pay regular dividends to shareholders.

Dividend investors prioritize stocks with consistent dividend payments and a history of dividend growth.

3.2 Key Features

Focus on companies with stable cash flows, strong financial health, and a commitment to returning capital to shareholders. Dividend investing can provide a source of passive income and potentially higher total returns over the long term.

4. Sector Investing

4.1 Definition

Sector investing involves allocating investments to specific sectors or industries of the economy.
Sector investors seek to capitalize on opportunities or trends within specific sectors that may outperform the broader market.

4.2 Key Features

Diversification across sectors helps reduce risk and exposure to individual companies or industries.
Sector investing requires research and analysis to identify sectors poised for growth or those that may benefit from specific economic or market conditions.

5. Alternative Investments

5.1 Definition

Alternative investments include a wide range of non-traditional asset classes beyond stocks, bonds, and cash. Examples of alternative investments include real estate, commodities, hedge funds, private equity, and venture capital.

5.2 Key Features

Alternative investments may offer diversification benefits, low correlation to traditional assets, and potential for higher returns.
Due diligence and understanding of the risks associated with alternative investments are essential before incorporating them into a portfolio.

6. Risk Management
6.1 Diversification

Diversification remains a fundamental principle in specialized investment strategies to reduce risk and optimize returns. Investors should consider combining different strategies or asset classes to achieve a well-rounded portfolio.

6.2 Due Diligence

Thorough research and analysis are critical when implementing specialized investment strategies to identify suitable opportunities and mitigate risks.
Consider consulting with financial professionals or advisors with expertise in specialized investment strategies for guidance and advice.

7. Conclusion

Specialized investment strategies offer unique opportunities for investors to tailor their portfolios to specific objectives, market conditions, or risk preferences. Whether pursuing value investing, growth investing, dividend investing, sector investing, or alternative investments, it's essential to understand the features, risks, and considerations associated with each strategy. By conducting thorough research, exercising due diligence, and diversifying effectively, investors can implement specialized investment strategies to enhance their investment outcomes and achieve their financial goals.

Chapter 25: Real Estate Investing

Real estate investing offers unique opportunities for building wealth, generating passive income, and diversifying investment portfolios. In this chapter, we'll explore the benefits of real estate investing, different types of real estate investments, and how to get started in the real estate market.

1. Benefits of Real Estate Investing
1.1 Potential for Appreciation

Real estate has the potential to appreciate in value over time, providing investors with capital appreciation and wealth accumulation opportunities.
1.2 Passive Income

Real estate investments, such as rental properties, can generate regular passive income through rental payments from tenants, offering a steady cash flow stream.

1.3 Diversification

Real estate investments offer diversification benefits by providing exposure to a tangible asset class with low correlation to stocks and bonds, helping to reduce overall portfolio risk.

1.4 Hedge Against Inflation

Real estate investments can serve as a hedge against inflation, as property values and rental income tend to increase with inflation over the long term.

2. Types of Real Estate Investments

2.1 Residential Real Estate

Residential real estate includes single-family homes, condominiums, townhouses, and multi-family properties. Residential properties can be rented out to tenants for income or flipped for short-term capital gains.

2.2 Commercial Real Estate

Commercial real estate encompasses properties used for business purposes, such as office buildings, retail centers, industrial warehouses, and multifamily apartment complexes. Commercial properties typically generate higher rental income but may require larger upfront investments and more management oversight.

2.3 Real Estate Investment Trusts (REITs)

REITs are publicly traded companies that own, operate, or finance income-generating real estate properties. REITs provide investors with a way to invest in real estate without directly owning physical properties and offer liquidity, diversification, and potentially high dividend yields.

2.4 Real Estate Crowdfunding

Real estate crowdfunding platforms allow individual investors to pool their capital and invest in real estate projects or properties.

Crowdfunding provides access to real estate investments with lower minimum investment requirements and offers opportunities for passive income and portfolio diversification.

3. How to Get Started in Real Estate

3.1 Educate Yourself

Start by educating yourself about the real estate market, investment strategies, and local market conditions.

Take advantage of resources such as books, online courses, seminars, and networking events to learn from experienced investors and industry professionals.

3.2 Set Investment Goals

Define your investment objectives, whether it's generating passive income, building equity, or achieving long-term capital appreciation.

Consider factors such as risk tolerance, investment horizon, and desired level of involvement in property management.

3.3 Build a Financial Plan

Assess your financial situation and develop a plan for funding your real estate investments.

Determine how much capital you can allocate to real estate, whether through savings, financing, or partnerships with other investors.

3.4 Start Small

Consider starting with a small investment property, such as a single-family home or condominium, to gain experience and learn the ropes of real estate investing.

As you gain confidence and expertise, you can gradually scale up your investments and diversify into different property types or investment strategies.

3.5 Conduct Due Diligence

Perform thorough due diligence on potential investment properties, including analyzing market trends, evaluating property fundamentals, and assessing financial metrics such as cash flow, cap rates, and return on investment (ROI).

3.6 Seek Professional Advice

Consider consulting with real estate agents, property managers, financial advisors, and legal professionals to help you navigate the complexities of real estate investing and make informed investment decisions.

4. Conclusion

Real estate investing offers numerous benefits, including potential for appreciation, passive income generation, diversification, and inflation hedging. Whether investing in residential properties, commercial real estate, REITs, or real estate crowdfunding, it's essential to educate yourself, set clear investment goals, and conduct thorough due diligence. By starting small, building a solid financial plan, and seeking professional advice when needed, investors can successfully enter the real estate market and build wealth over the long term.

Chapter 26: Cryptocurrency Investing

Cryptocurrency investing has gained significant popularity in recent years, offering investors opportunities for potential high returns and diversification. In this chapter, we'll provide an overview of cryptocurrencies, discuss the benefits and risks of investing in them, and explore how to buy, store, and sell cryptocurrencies.

1. Overview of Cryptocurrencies
1.1 Definition

Cryptocurrencies are digital or virtual currencies that use cryptography for security and operate on decentralized networks called blockchains.

Bitcoin, Ethereum, and Ripple are some of the most well-known cryptocurrencies, but thousands of others exist, each with its own unique features and use cases.

1.2 Key Features

Decentralization: Cryptocurrencies are decentralized, meaning they are not controlled by any central authority, such as a government or financial institution.

Blockchain Technology: Transactions on cryptocurrency networks are recorded on a public ledger called a blockchain, which ensures transparency, security, and immutability.

Limited Supply: Many cryptocurrencies have a fixed or capped supply, meaning there is a maximum number of coins that can ever be created, which can impact their value over time.

2. Benefits and Risks of Investing in Cryptocurrencies

2.1 Benefits

Potential for High Returns: Cryptocurrencies have generated significant returns for investors in the past, with some experiencing exponential growth in value.

Diversification: Cryptocurrencies offer diversification benefits, as they have low correlation with traditional asset classes such as stocks and bonds.

Innovation: Cryptocurrencies are at the forefront of technological innovation, with the potential to disrupt various industries and create new economic models.

2.2 Risks

Volatility: Cryptocurrencies are highly volatile and can experience significant price fluctuations in a short period, which can lead to substantial gains or losses for investors.

Regulatory Uncertainty: Regulatory uncertainty surrounding cryptocurrencies can impact their adoption and value, as governments around the world grapple with how to regulate them.

Security Risks: Cryptocurrency exchanges and wallets are susceptible to hacking and cyber attacks, leading to the loss of investor funds.

3. How to Buy, Store, and Sell Cryptocurrencies

3.1 Buying Cryptocurrencies

Choose a Cryptocurrency Exchange: Select a reputable cryptocurrency exchange where you can buy, sell, and trade cryptocurrencies. Popular exchanges include Coinbase, Binance, and Kraken.

Create an Account: Sign up for an account on the chosen exchange and complete the verification process, which may require providing personal information and identity verification.

Deposit Funds: Deposit fiat currency (e.g., USD, EUR) into your exchange account using bank transfers, credit/debit cards, or other payment methods.

Place an Order: Once your account is funded, you can place buy orders for the desired cryptocurrencies, specifying the amount and price at which you wish to buy.

3.2 Storing Cryptocurrencies

Choose a Wallet: Select a cryptocurrency wallet to securely store your digital assets. Wallets come in various forms, including hardware wallets, software wallets, and mobile wallets.

Transfer Cryptocurrencies: Transfer the cryptocurrencies purchased on the exchange to your chosen wallet for long-term storage and security. Be sure to keep your private keys safe and secure, as they provide access to your funds.

3.3 Selling Cryptocurrencies

Choose an Exchange: To sell cryptocurrencies, log in to your chosen cryptocurrency exchange and navigate to the trading section.

Place a Sell Order: Specify the amount and price at which you wish to sell your cryptocurrencies, and place a sell order on the exchange.

Withdraw Funds: Once your sell order is executed, you can withdraw the proceeds in fiat currency to your bank account or keep them on the exchange for future trading.

4. Conclusion

Cryptocurrency investing offers unique opportunities for potential high returns, diversification, and participation in technological innovation. However, it also comes with risks, including volatility, regulatory uncertainty, and security concerns. By understanding the fundamentals of cryptocurrencies, evaluating the benefits and risks, and following best practices for buying, storing, and selling cryptocurrencies, investors can make informed decisions and navigate the dynamic world of cryptocurrency investing effectively. Remember to conduct thorough research, exercise caution, and only invest what you can afford to lose in the cryptocurrency market.

Chapter 27: Online Business Models

The internet has revolutionized the way businesses operate, opening up a myriad of opportunities for entrepreneurs to start and grow online ventures. In this chapter, we'll explore various online business models, their features, and considerations for launching and scaling successful online businesses.

1. E-commerce
1.1 Definition

E-commerce involves buying and selling goods or services online through websites, online marketplaces, or social media platforms.
E-commerce businesses can range from small, niche online stores to large, multinational retailers.
1.2 Key Features

Product-Based: E-commerce businesses sell physical or digital products to customers, ranging from consumer goods to digital downloads.

Online Payment Processing: E-commerce platforms integrate payment gateways to facilitate secure online transactions, such as credit/debit card payments, digital wallets, and other payment methods.

Logistics and Fulfillment: E-commerce businesses must manage shipping, inventory, and fulfillment processes to deliver products to customers efficiently.

2. Subscription Services

2.1 Definition

Subscription services offer access to products or content on a recurring basis in exchange for a subscription fee. Subscription-based business models have gained popularity across various industries, including media streaming, software as a service (SaaS), and subscription boxes.

2.2 Key Features

Recurring Revenue: Subscription businesses generate predictable recurring revenue streams, providing stability and scalability for long-term growth.

Customer Retention: By offering ongoing value and personalized experiences, subscription services can enhance customer loyalty and retention.

Content Curation: Subscription services curate content or products tailored to the preferences and interests of subscribers, creating a personalized experience.

3. Digital Products and Services

3.1 Definition

Digital products and services are intangible goods or services that can be delivered electronically over the internet. Examples include e-books, online courses, software applications, digital downloads, and freelance services.

3.2 Key Features

Scalability: Digital products and services can be replicated and delivered to an unlimited number of customers without incurring additional production costs.

Low Overhead: Digital businesses often have lower overhead costs compared to traditional brick-and-mortar businesses, making them accessible to entrepreneurs with limited resources.

Global Reach: Digital products and services have a global reach, allowing businesses to target customers worldwide and expand their market reach.

4. Affiliate Marketing

4.1 Definition

Affiliate marketing involves promoting third-party products or services and earning a commission for each sale or referral generated through affiliate links.

Affiliate marketers leverage websites, blogs, social media, and other online channels to drive traffic and generate sales for affiliate partners.

4.2 Key Features

Performance-Based: Affiliate marketing is performance-based, meaning affiliates earn commissions based on their performance in driving sales or referrals.

Low Barrier to Entry: Affiliate marketing requires minimal upfront investment or product development, making it accessible to beginners and individuals looking to monetize online traffic.

Diverse Revenue Streams: Affiliate marketers can diversify their revenue streams by promoting products across different niches and industries, earning commissions from multiple affiliate programs.

5. Online Advertising

5.1 Definition

Online advertising involves displaying promotional messages or advertisements to target audiences through digital channels such as websites, search engines, social media, and mobile apps.

Businesses can utilize various online advertising platforms, including pay-per-click (PPC) advertising, display ads, native advertising, and sponsored content.

5.2 Key Features

Targeted Advertising: Online advertising platforms offer advanced targeting options, allowing businesses to reach specific demographics, interests, and behaviors with precision.

Measurable Results: Online advertising provides real-time analytics and performance metrics, enabling businesses to track the effectiveness of their ad campaigns and optimize for better results.

Cost-Effective: Compared to traditional advertising methods, online advertising can be more cost-effective, with flexible budgeting options and the ability to reach a wider audience at lower costs.

6. Considerations for Launching an Online Business

6.1 Market Research: Conduct thorough market research to identify niche opportunities, understand customer needs and preferences, and assess competition in the target market.

6.2 Business Plan: Develop a comprehensive business plan outlining your business model, target audience, marketing strategies, revenue streams, and financial projections.

6.3 Website and Online Presence: Invest in building a professional website, optimizing for search engines (SEO), and establishing a strong online presence across relevant digital channels.

6.4 Customer Acquisition: Implement effective customer acquisition strategies, such as content marketing, social media marketing, email marketing, and search engine optimization (SEO), to attract and engage your target audience.

6.5 Monetization Strategies: Identify and implement monetization strategies aligned with your business model, such as e-commerce sales, subscription fees, advertising revenue, affiliate commissions, or digital product sales.

6.6 Legal and Regulatory Compliance: Ensure compliance with relevant laws and regulations governing online businesses, including data protection, privacy, intellectual property, and taxation.

7. Conclusion

Online business models offer diverse opportunities for entrepreneurs to start and grow successful ventures in the digital economy. Whether launching an e-commerce store, subscription service, digital product, affiliate marketing business, or online advertising platform, it's essential to understand the features, benefits, and considerations associated with each model. By conducting thorough research, developing a solid business plan, and implementing effective strategies for customer acquisition and monetization, entrepreneurs can build thriving online businesses and capitalize on the vast opportunities available in the digital marketplace.

Chapter 28: Dropshipping

Dropshipping has become a popular business model for entrepreneurs looking to start an online retail business with minimal upfront investment and inventory management. In this chapter, we'll explore what dropshipping is, how to set up a dropshipping business, and strategies for finding and managing suppliers effectively.

1. What is Dropshipping?
1.1 Definition

Dropshipping is a retail fulfillment method where a store doesn't keep the products it sells in stock. Instead, when a store sells a product, it purchases the item from a third party and has it shipped directly to the customer.
The merchant (dropshipper) acts as a middleman, handling customer orders, while the supplier or manufacturer fulfills and ships the orders directly to the end customer.
1.2 Key Features

Low Upfront Investment: Dropshipping requires minimal upfront investment compared to traditional retail models since there's no need to purchase inventory in advance.
No Inventory Management: Dropshippers don't need to handle or store inventory, reducing overhead costs and logistical complexities.
Scalability: Dropshipping businesses can scale quickly and easily by adding new products or suppliers without the constraints of physical inventory.
2. How to Set Up a Dropshipping Business
2.1 Choose a Niche

Select a niche market or product category based on market research, competition analysis, and personal interests or expertise.
2.2 Research Suppliers

Identify reliable and reputable suppliers or manufacturers willing to dropship products for your business.
Consider factors such as product quality, pricing, shipping times, and customer service when evaluating potential suppliers.
2.3 Set Up an Online Store

Create an e-commerce website or online store to showcase your products and facilitate online transactions.
Choose an e-commerce platform such as Shopify, WooCommerce, or Magento that offers dropshipping integration and customization options.
2.4 Source Products

Curate a selection of products from your chosen suppliers and add them to your online store.
Optimize product listings with high-quality images, detailed descriptions, and competitive pricing to attract customers.

2.5 Establish Pricing and Profit Margins

Determine pricing strategies and profit margins for your products, taking into account supplier costs, shipping fees, and other overhead expenses.
Set competitive prices that offer value to customers while ensuring profitability for your business.

2.6 Implement Marketing Strategies

Develop marketing strategies to drive traffic to your online store and generate sales.
Utilize digital marketing channels such as social media, search engine optimization (SEO), email marketing, and influencer partnerships to reach your target audience.

3. Finding and Managing Suppliers

3.1 Research and Vetting

Research potential suppliers thoroughly, seeking recommendations, reading reviews, and contacting them directly to discuss partnership opportunities.
Vet suppliers based on criteria such as product quality, reliability, responsiveness, and fulfillment capabilities.

3.2 Negotiation and Agreements

Negotiate terms and agreements with suppliers, including pricing, shipping terms, return policies, and order fulfillment procedures.
Formalize agreements through contracts or written agreements to clarify expectations and protect both parties' interests.

3.3 Communication and Relationship Management

Maintain open and transparent communication with suppliers to address any issues, provide feedback, and ensure smooth order processing and fulfillment.

Build and nurture strong relationships with suppliers through regular communication, mutual respect, and collaboration to foster long-term partnerships.

3.4 Performance Monitoring

Monitor supplier performance regularly to assess reliability, fulfillment accuracy, shipping times, and customer satisfaction.

Implement performance metrics and KPIs to track supplier performance and identify areas for improvement or optimization.

4. Conclusion

Dropshipping offers entrepreneurs a flexible and low-risk way to start an online retail business without the need for significant upfront investment or inventory management. By understanding the dropshipping model, conducting thorough research, and implementing effective strategies for finding and managing suppliers, entrepreneurs can build successful dropshipping businesses and capitalize on the vast opportunities available in the e-commerce market. Remember to prioritize customer satisfaction, continuously optimize your operations, and adapt to evolving market trends to thrive in the competitive dropshipping landscape.

Chapter 29: Affiliate Marketing

Affiliate marketing is a performance-based marketing strategy where individuals or businesses earn commissions by promoting products or services of other companies. In this chapter, we'll provide an introduction to affiliate marketing, discuss how to choose profitable niches, and explore strategies for effectively promoting affiliate products.

1. Introduction to Affiliate Marketing
1.1 Definition

Affiliate marketing involves promoting third-party products or services through affiliate links and earning commissions for successful referrals or sales.
Affiliates (also known as publishers or marketers) promote products to their audience through various online channels, such as websites, blogs, social media, email, and video content.
1.2 Key Players

Merchants or Advertisers: Companies or businesses that offer affiliate programs and provide products or services for promotion.

Affiliates: Individuals or entities that promote products or services through affiliate links and earn commissions for driving traffic or sales.

Affiliate Networks: Platforms that connect merchants with affiliates and facilitate tracking, reporting, and payment processes for affiliate programs.

2. How to Choose Profitable Niches

2.1 Research Market Demand

Identify niche markets with high demand and low competition by conducting market research, keyword analysis, and competitor analysis.

Look for trends, consumer interests, and pain points within specific niches to identify lucrative opportunities for affiliate marketing.

2.2 Assess Profitability

Evaluate the profitability of potential niches based on factors such as product pricing, commission rates, average order value (AOV), and customer lifetime value (CLV).

Choose niches with products or services that offer attractive commission rates and have a higher potential for generating significant affiliate earnings.

2.3 Consider Audience Interests

Align niche selection with the interests, preferences, and needs of your target audience to ensure relevance and engagement.

Choose niches that resonate with your audience's demographics, psychographics, and purchasing behavior to maximize conversion rates and affiliate income.

3. Strategies for Promoting Affiliate Products

3.1 Content Marketing

Create high-quality, informative content that educates, entertains, or solves problems for your audience.
Incorporate affiliate links naturally within your content, such as product reviews, tutorials, comparisons, and recommendations.

3.2 Search Engine Optimization (SEO)

Optimize your website or content for search engines to improve visibility and attract organic traffic.
Target relevant keywords and optimize meta tags, headings, and content structure to rank higher in search engine results pages (SERPs).

3.3 Social Media Marketing

Leverage social media platforms to promote affiliate products and engage with your audience.
Share compelling content, product recommendations, and promotional offers on social media channels such as Facebook, Instagram, Twitter, LinkedIn, and Pinterest.

3.4 Email Marketing

Build an email list of subscribers interested in your niche or industry.
Send targeted email campaigns featuring affiliate products, exclusive offers, and valuable content to nurture relationships and drive conversions.

3.5 Influencer Partnerships

Collaborate with influencers or bloggers in your niche to reach a broader audience and increase credibility.
Partner with influencers to create sponsored content, product reviews, or affiliate promotions that resonate with their followers and drive conversions.

3.6 Paid Advertising

Invest in paid advertising channels such as pay-per-click (PPC) advertising, display ads, or native advertising to drive targeted traffic to affiliate offers.

Set clear objectives, target audience segments effectively, and optimize ad campaigns for maximum ROI and conversion rates.

4. Conclusion

Affiliate marketing offers a lucrative opportunity for individuals and businesses to monetize their online presence and generate passive income by promoting third-party products or services. By choosing profitable niches, conducting thorough research, and implementing effective promotion strategies, affiliates can maximize their earning potential and build successful affiliate marketing businesses. Remember to focus on providing value to your audience, building trust and credibility, and continuously optimizing your marketing efforts to achieve long-term success in affiliate marketing.

Chapter 30: Additional Income Streams

In addition to traditional employment or primary business ventures, diversifying income streams can provide financial stability, flexibility, and opportunities for wealth accumulation. In this chapter, we'll explore various additional income streams that individuals can pursue to supplement their earnings and achieve financial goals.

1. Freelancing or Consulting
1.1 Definition

Freelancing or consulting involves offering your skills, expertise, or services on a contract basis to clients or businesses.
Freelancers and consultants work independently, providing services such as writing, graphic design, web development, marketing, consulting, and more.
1.2 Key Features

Flexibility: Freelancing offers flexibility in terms of schedule, workload, and client selection, allowing individuals to work on projects that align with their interests and availability.

Potential for High Earnings: Experienced freelancers and consultants can command higher rates for their specialized skills and expertise, leading to lucrative income opportunities.
Diverse Clientele: Freelancers and consultants can work with a diverse range of clients across industries, gaining exposure to different projects, challenges, and opportunities.

2. Rental Income

2.1 Definition

Rental income is earned by leasing out properties such as residential real estate, commercial spaces, vacation rentals, or storage units to tenants.
Property owners earn rental income through monthly rent payments from tenants, providing a passive income stream.

2.2 Key Features

Passive Income: Rental income provides a passive stream of income for property owners, requiring minimal ongoing involvement once properties are rented out.
Appreciation Potential: Real estate properties have the potential to appreciate in value over time, increasing the equity and overall value of the investment.
Tax Benefits: Property owners may benefit from tax deductions such as mortgage interest, property taxes, depreciation, and maintenance expenses, reducing taxable income.

3. Investing in Dividend-Paying Stocks

3.1 Definition

Dividend-paying stocks are shares of publicly traded companies that distribute a portion of their profits to shareholders in the form of dividends.
Dividends are typically paid out on a quarterly basis and provide investors with regular income payments.

3.2 Key Features

Passive Income: Dividend-paying stocks offer a passive income stream for investors, providing regular dividend payments without the need for active involvement.

Potential for Growth: Investors can benefit from both dividend income and capital appreciation as stock prices increase over time.

Diversification: Investing in dividend-paying stocks allows investors to diversify their portfolios and mitigate risk by spreading investments across different companies and industries.

4. Online Courses or Digital Products

4.1 Definition

Online courses or digital products are educational or informational materials that are created and sold online, such as e-books, online courses, webinars, templates, and digital downloads.

Creators earn income by selling access to their digital products to customers or subscribers.

4.2 Key Features

Scalability: Online courses and digital products can be created once and sold to an unlimited number of customers, providing scalable income opportunities.

Passive Income: Once created, digital products can generate passive income through sales, requiring minimal ongoing maintenance or updates.

Expertise Monetization: Creators can monetize their knowledge, skills, or expertise by creating valuable educational content that addresses the needs and interests of their target audience.

5. Peer-to-Peer Lending

5.1 Definition

Peer-to-peer (P2P) lending platforms connect individual borrowers with investors willing to lend money in exchange for interest payments.

Investors earn income through interest payments on loans provided to borrowers through P2P lending platforms.

5.2 Key Features

Diversification: P2P lending allows investors to diversify their investment portfolios by allocating funds across a portfolio of loans to minimize risk.

Passive Income: Investors earn passive income through regular interest payments from borrowers, providing a steady stream of income over time.

Access to Credit Markets: P2P lending platforms provide investors with access to credit markets and the opportunity to earn competitive returns outside of traditional investment options.

6. Conclusion

Diversifying income streams through additional sources of earnings can enhance financial stability, provide flexibility, and accelerate progress towards achieving financial goals. Whether through freelancing, rental income, dividend-paying stocks, online courses, or peer-to-peer lending, individuals can leverage various income streams to supplement their primary sources of income and build wealth over time. By exploring opportunities, investing wisely, and actively managing additional income streams, individuals can create a robust financial foundation and work towards financial independence and security.

Chapter 31: Side Hustles

Side hustles have become increasingly popular as individuals seek to supplement their primary income, pursue passions, or achieve financial goals. In this chapter, we'll explore the definition and benefits of side hustles, popular side hustle ideas, and strategies for effectively managing multiple income streams.

1. Definition and Benefits of Side Hustles
1.1 Definition

A side hustle refers to any additional work or income-generating activity that individuals pursue alongside their primary job or business.
Side hustles can take various forms, including freelancing, consulting, e-commerce, gig work, part-time jobs, and creative endeavors.
1.2 Benefits

Supplemental Income: Side hustles provide an additional source of income beyond primary earnings, helping individuals meet financial needs, pay off debt, or save for goals.
Skill Development: Side hustles offer opportunities for skill development, learning new technologies, and gaining experience in different industries or roles.

Flexibility: Side hustles often offer flexibility in terms of schedule, workload, and location, allowing individuals to work on their own terms and balance other commitments.
Passion Pursuit: Side hustles allow individuals to pursue passions, interests, or hobbies outside of their primary job, providing fulfillment and creative expression.

2. Popular Side Hustle Ideas

2.1 Freelancing or Consulting

Offer your skills, expertise, or services on a contract basis to clients or businesses.
Examples include writing, graphic design, web development, marketing, consulting, and coaching.

2.2 E-commerce or Dropshipping

Start an online store or dropshipping business to sell products to customers.
Explore niche markets, source products, and promote your store through digital marketing channels.

2.3 Gig Economy Work

Join gig economy platforms such as Uber, Lyft, TaskRabbit, or Upwork to provide services on a freelance or part-time basis.
Offer services such as ridesharing, delivery, errand running, virtual assistance, or freelance projects.

2.4 Content Creation

Create and monetize content through blogging, vlogging, podcasting, or social media.
Generate income through advertising, sponsorships, affiliate marketing, or selling digital products.

2.5 Rental Income

Rent out properties such as residential real estate, vacation rentals, or storage units to tenants.

Explore platforms such as Airbnb, VRBO, or SpareFoot to list and manage rental properties.

3. How to Manage Multiple Income Streams

3.1 Prioritize and Organize

Prioritize income streams based on their importance, earning potential, and alignment with your goals.

Organize your schedule, tasks, and responsibilities to effectively balance multiple income streams and avoid overwhelm.

3.2 Set Clear Goals and Boundaries

Define clear goals and objectives for each income stream, such as income targets, growth milestones, or skill development objectives.

Set boundaries to manage workload, avoid burnout, and maintain work-life balance while juggling multiple commitments.

3.3 Time Management and Productivity

Use time management techniques and productivity tools to optimize your workflow and maximize efficiency.

Allocate dedicated time blocks for each income stream, set deadlines, and prioritize tasks to stay focused and productive.

3.4 Automate and Delegate

Automate repetitive tasks, streamline processes, and leverage technology to save time and resources.

Delegate tasks or outsource responsibilities where possible to free up your time and focus on high-impact activities.

3.5 Monitor and Evaluate Performance

Regularly monitor the performance of each income stream, track earnings, and assess progress towards your goals.

Evaluate the effectiveness of your strategies, identify areas for improvement, and make adjustments as needed to optimize results.

4. Conclusion

Side hustles offer individuals opportunities to supplement their income, pursue passions, and achieve financial goals outside of their primary job or business. Whether through freelancing, e-commerce, gig work, content creation, or rental income, individuals can leverage various side hustle ideas to diversify income streams and create additional sources of revenue. By prioritizing, organizing, setting clear goals, managing time effectively, and monitoring performance, individuals can successfully manage multiple income streams and unlock the benefits of side hustles while maintaining work-life balance and achieving financial success.

Chapter 32: Freelancing

Freelancing offers individuals the flexibility to work independently, pursue their passions, and earn income by providing services to clients on a contract basis. In this chapter, we'll provide an overview of freelancing opportunities, discuss how to build a freelancing portfolio, and explore strategies for finding clients and setting rates.

1. Overview of Freelancing Opportunities
1.1 Diverse Skill Sets

Freelancing opportunities span a wide range of industries, skill sets, and expertise areas.
Common freelancing categories include writing, graphic design, web development, marketing, consulting, photography, virtual assistance, and more.
1.2 Remote Work Trends

The rise of remote work and digital connectivity has fueled the growth of freelancing opportunities globally. Freelancers can work with clients from anywhere in the world, leveraging technology to collaborate, communicate, and deliver services remotely.
1.3 Gig Economy Platforms

Gig economy platforms such as Upwork, Freelancer, Fiverr, and TaskRabbit connect freelancers with clients seeking services on a project basis.

These platforms offer a marketplace for freelancers to showcase their skills, find job opportunities, and secure contracts with clients.

2. Building a Freelancing Portfolio

2.1 Showcase Your Skills

Create a professional portfolio showcasing your skills, expertise, and previous work samples.
Include a variety of samples that demonstrate your capabilities and the range of services you offer.

2.2 Develop a Personal Brand

Define your unique value proposition and brand identity as a freelancer.
Create a professional website, logo, and branding materials to establish a strong online presence and attract clients.

2.3 Gain Experience

Gain practical experience and build your portfolio by working on projects, volunteering, or offering discounted services to early clients.
Focus on delivering high-quality work, exceeding client expectations, and collecting testimonials and references for future use.

3. Finding Clients and Setting Rates

3.1 Networking and Referrals

Leverage your professional network and connections to find potential clients and opportunities.
Attend industry events, join online communities, and participate in networking activities to expand your reach and visibility.

3.2 Online Platforms

Create profiles on freelancing platforms and marketplaces to showcase your services and attract clients.

Optimize your profiles with relevant keywords, skills, and portfolio samples to increase visibility and searchability.

3.3 Marketing and Promotion

Market your services through digital channels such as social media, content marketing, email newsletters, and blogging.
Share valuable content, industry insights, and success stories to demonstrate your expertise and attract potential clients.

3.4 Setting Rates

Research industry standards, market rates, and competitor pricing to determine your freelance rates.
Consider factors such as your experience, expertise, niche specialization, project scope, and client budget when setting rates.
Calculate your desired hourly rate or project-based pricing to ensure fair compensation for your time, skills, and value provided.

4. Conclusion

Freelancing offers individuals the opportunity to work independently, pursue their passions, and earn income by providing services to clients on a contract basis. By leveraging diverse skill sets, building a strong freelancing portfolio, and effectively marketing services, freelancers can attract clients, secure projects, and build successful freelance careers. By networking, promoting services, and setting competitive rates, freelancers can establish themselves as valuable service providers, expand their client base, and achieve financial success in the freelancing industry.

Chapter 33: E-commerce

E-commerce has transformed the way businesses operate and revolutionized the shopping experience for consumers worldwide. In this chapter, we'll explore how to start an e-commerce business, choose the right products to sell, and strategies for marketing and growing your e-commerce store.

1. Starting an E-commerce Business
1.1 Business Plan

Define your e-commerce business concept, target market, and unique selling proposition (USP).
Conduct market research to identify niche opportunities, analyze competitors, and understand consumer preferences and trends.
1.2 Choose an E-commerce Platform

Select an e-commerce platform that meets your business needs, budget, and technical requirements.
Popular e-commerce platforms include Shopify, WooCommerce, Magento, BigCommerce, and Squarespace.
1.3 Set Up Your Online Store

Design and customize your e-commerce website to reflect your brand identity and create a seamless shopping experience for customers.
Optimize your website for mobile responsiveness, fast loading times, and intuitive navigation to enhance user experience.

1.4 Secure Payment Processing

Integrate secure payment gateways to accept online payments from customers.

Offer multiple payment options, including credit/debit cards, digital wallets, and alternative payment methods, to accommodate diverse customer preferences.

2. Choosing the Right Products to Sell

2.1 Identify Market Demand

Research market trends, consumer behavior, and product demand to identify profitable product categories or niches.

Use keyword research tools, trend analysis, and competitor research to assess market demand and competition levels.

2.2 Product Selection Criteria

Choose products that align with your target market's needs, preferences, and pain points.

Consider factors such as product uniqueness, quality, pricing, profit margins, shipping logistics, and potential for scalability.

2.3 Test and Validate Products

Test market demand and validate product ideas through market research, prototype testing, and pre-launch surveys.

Start with a small product catalog or conduct pilot launches to gauge customer interest and feedback before scaling up.

3. Marketing and Growing Your E-commerce Store

3.1 Search Engine Optimization (SEO)

Optimize your website and product pages for search engines to improve visibility and organic traffic.

Conduct keyword research, optimize meta tags, headings, and product descriptions, and build high-quality backlinks to improve search rankings.

3.2 Content Marketing

Create valuable content such as blog posts, articles, tutorials, and videos to engage your audience and drive traffic to your e-commerce store.

Share content on social media, email newsletters, and other digital channels to attract and retain customers.

3.3 Social Media Marketing

Leverage social media platforms such as Facebook, Instagram, Twitter, Pinterest, and LinkedIn to promote your products and engage with your audience.

Create compelling visual content, run targeted ads, and engage with followers to build brand awareness and drive sales.

3.4 Email Marketing

Build an email list of subscribers and customers to nurture relationships and drive repeat purchases.

Send personalized email campaigns, product recommendations, and promotional offers to encourage conversions and increase customer loyalty.

3.5 Influencer Partnerships

Collaborate with influencers, bloggers, and content creators in your niche to reach a wider audience and build credibility.

Partner with influencers to create sponsored content, product reviews, or influencer campaigns that resonate with their followers and drive sales.

4. Conclusion

Starting and growing an e-commerce business requires careful planning, strategic execution, and continuous adaptation to market trends and consumer preferences. By selecting the right products to sell, leveraging effective marketing strategies, and providing exceptional customer experiences, e-commerce entrepreneurs can build successful online stores and achieve long-term growth and profitability. By staying informed, staying agile, and staying customer-focused, you can navigate the dynamic e-commerce landscape and capitalize on the vast opportunities available in the digital marketplace.

Chapter 34: Financial Independence

Financial independence, often referred to as FI, is a state of financial well-being where individuals have sufficient passive income to cover their living expenses without the need for active employment. In this chapter, we'll explore the concept of financial independence, strategies for achieving it, and the benefits of attaining financial freedom.

1. Understanding Financial Independence
1.1 Definition

Financial independence is the ability to sustain one's lifestyle without relying on a traditional job or paycheck.
It involves having enough passive income, such as investments, rental income, or business profits, to cover living expenses and achieve financial goals.
1.2 Components of Financial Independence

Passive Income: Income generated from investments, rental properties, royalties, or business ventures that does not require active involvement.

Expense Management: Conscious spending habits, budgeting, and frugality to minimize expenses and maximize savings.

Asset Accumulation: Building wealth through investments, savings, and assets that generate income and appreciate over time.

2. Strategies for Achieving Financial Independence

2.1 Save and Invest Wisely

Prioritize saving and investing a portion of your income regularly to build wealth and generate passive income.

Utilize tax-advantaged accounts such as 401(k) plans, IRAs, and HSAs to maximize investment returns and reduce tax liabilities.

2.2 Reduce Debt

Pay off high-interest debt aggressively to free up cash flow and accelerate wealth accumulation.

Adopt debt repayment strategies such as the debt snowball or debt avalanche method to prioritize and eliminate debts systematically.

2.3 Diversify Income Streams

Create multiple streams of income through investments, rental properties, freelancing, entrepreneurship, or passive business ventures.

Diversify income sources to mitigate risk and increase resilience against economic downturns or job loss.

2.4 Live Below Your Means

Adopt a frugal lifestyle and practice mindful spending to reduce expenses and increase savings.

Differentiate between needs and wants, prioritize essential expenses, and avoid lifestyle inflation to maintain financial stability.

2.5 Invest in Income-Generating Assets

Allocate investments into income-generating assets such as dividend-paying stocks, real estate investment trusts (REITs), rental properties, or business ventures.

Focus on assets that provide steady cash flow and long-term appreciation potential to support financial independence goals.

3. Benefits of Financial Independence

3.1 Freedom and Flexibility

Achieving financial independence provides freedom and flexibility to pursue passions, interests, or hobbies without the constraints of a traditional job.

Individuals can choose how to allocate their time, energy, and resources based on personal priorities and values.

3.2 Reduced Stress and Anxiety

Financial independence reduces financial stress and anxiety associated with job insecurity, debt, or living paycheck to paycheck.

Individuals can enjoy peace of mind knowing they have sufficient resources to support themselves and their families.

3.3 Legacy and Impact

Financial independence allows individuals to leave a legacy, make a positive impact, and contribute to causes they care about.

By achieving financial freedom, individuals can support charitable initiatives, mentor others, or pursue philanthropic endeavors to create a lasting impact in their communities and beyond.

4. Conclusion

Financial independence is a goal worth pursuing for individuals seeking autonomy, security, and fulfillment in their lives. By adopting strategic financial habits, saving and investing wisely, and diversifying income streams, individuals can pave the path towards financial independence and unlock a world of opportunities. Whether it's retiring early, pursuing passion projects, or making a difference in the world, financial independence empowers individuals to live life on their own terms and create a meaningful legacy for themselves and future generations.

Chapter 35: Budgeting for Financial Success

Budgeting is a fundamental aspect of personal finance that helps individuals manage their money effectively, achieve financial goals, and attain long-term financial success. In this chapter, we'll explore strategies for creating and sticking to a budget, tools and apps for budgeting, and the importance of long-term financial planning.

1. Creating and Sticking to a Budget
1.1 Assess Your Finances

Start by evaluating your income, expenses, assets, and liabilities to gain a clear understanding of your financial situation.
Track your spending habits and identify areas where you can cut back or optimize expenses.
1.2 Set Financial Goals

Define short-term, medium-term, and long-term financial goals based on your priorities, values, and aspirations. Establish SMART (Specific, Measurable, Achievable, Relevant, Time-bound) goals to provide clarity and motivation for budgeting.

1.3 Create a Budget

Develop a comprehensive budget that allocates income towards essential expenses, savings, debt repayment, and discretionary spending categories.
Use budgeting methods such as zero-based budgeting, envelope budgeting, or percentage-based budgeting to allocate funds effectively.

1.4 Track and Monitor Expenses

Regularly track your expenses and compare them against your budget to ensure you're staying on track.
Use expense tracking tools, spreadsheets, or budgeting apps to monitor spending in real-time and identify areas for improvement.

1.5 Adjust and Adapt

Be flexible and willing to adjust your budget as circumstances change or unexpected expenses arise.
Review your budget regularly and make necessary adjustments to accommodate changes in income, expenses, or financial goals.

2. Tools and Apps for Budgeting

2.1 Personal Finance Apps

Utilize personal finance apps such as Mint, YNAB (You Need a Budget), Personal Capital, or PocketGuard to track expenses, create budgets, and monitor financial goals.

These apps offer features such as expense categorization, goal tracking, bill reminders, and financial insights to help users manage their money effectively.

2.2 Budgeting Spreadsheets

Create custom budgeting spreadsheets using Microsoft Excel, Google Sheets, or other spreadsheet software to tailor budgeting templates to your specific needs.

Customize columns for income, expenses, savings goals, and debt payments, and use formulas to calculate totals and track progress over time.

2.3 Envelope Systems

Adopt digital envelope systems such as Goodbudget or Mvelopes to allocate funds into virtual envelopes for different spending categories.

These systems mimic the traditional envelope budgeting method by helping users allocate and track funds for specific purposes while providing visibility into available balances.

3. Long-Term Financial Planning

3.1 Retirement Planning

Develop a retirement savings plan and contribute regularly to retirement accounts such as 401(k) plans, IRAs, or pension schemes.

Estimate retirement expenses, set savings targets, and consider factors such as investment returns, inflation, and longevity when planning for retirement.

3.2 Emergency Fund

Build an emergency fund to cover unexpected expenses or financial setbacks such as job loss, medical emergencies, or major home repairs.

Aim to save three to six months' worth of living expenses in a liquid savings account or high-yield savings account for financial security.

3.3 Investment Strategies

Diversify investments across asset classes such as stocks, bonds, mutual funds, real estate, and alternative investments to mitigate risk and achieve long-term growth.
Consider factors such as risk tolerance, time horizon, and investment objectives when selecting investment vehicles and asset allocation strategies.

3.4 Estate Planning

Develop an estate plan that includes essential documents such as a will, trust, power of attorney, and healthcare directives to protect assets and ensure wishes are carried out.
Review and update your estate plan regularly to reflect changes in family dynamics, financial circumstances, or legal requirements.

4. Conclusion

Budgeting is a foundational tool for achieving financial success and building a secure future. By creating and sticking to a budget, utilizing budgeting tools and apps, and incorporating long-term financial planning strategies, individuals can take control of their finances, achieve financial goals, and build wealth over time. Whether it's managing day-to-day expenses, saving for retirement, or planning for major life events, budgeting empowers individuals to make informed financial decisions and create a solid foundation for long-term financial stability and prosperity.

Chapter 36: Achieving Financial Independence

Financial independence is a significant milestone that offers individuals the freedom to pursue their passions, live life on their own terms, and achieve lasting prosperity. In this chapter, we'll explore the principles of financial independence, strategies for reducing expenses and increasing savings, and tips for building and maintaining wealth.

1. Principles of Financial Independence
1.1 Live Below Your Means

Spend less than you earn and prioritize saving and investing to build wealth over time.

Adopt a frugal lifestyle, differentiate between needs and wants, and avoid lifestyle inflation to maintain financial stability.

1.2 Invest Wisely

Allocate investments strategically across asset classes such as stocks, bonds, real estate, and alternative investments to generate passive income and achieve long-term growth. Diversify investments to mitigate risk and capitalize on opportunities in various market conditions.

1.3 Avoid Debt

Minimize debt and prioritize debt repayment to reduce interest expenses and free up cash flow for savings and investments.

Use debt strategically for assets that appreciate in value, such as education, real estate, or business investments, while avoiding high-interest consumer debt.

1.4 Continuously Educate Yourself

Stay informed about personal finance principles, investment strategies, and market trends to make informed financial decisions.

Invest in financial literacy, attend seminars, read books, and seek advice from trusted financial professionals to enhance your financial knowledge and skills.

2. Strategies for Reducing Expenses and Increasing Savings

2.1 Budgeting and Expense Tracking

Create a budget that aligns with your financial goals and values, and track expenses regularly to identify areas for improvement.

Use budgeting tools, apps, or spreadsheets to monitor spending, set limits, and prioritize saving and investing.

2.2 Minimize Discretionary Spending

Limit discretionary expenses such as dining out, entertainment, travel, and impulse purchases to reduce unnecessary spending.

Set spending limits, practice mindful spending, and prioritize experiences over material possessions to maximize enjoyment and savings.

2.3 Negotiate and Shop Smart

Negotiate bills, contracts, and subscriptions to lower costs and save money on recurring expenses.

Comparison shop, look for discounts, coupons, and promotions, and buy in bulk or secondhand to maximize savings on essential purchases.

2.4 Cut Housing Costs

Explore housing alternatives such as downsizing, renting, house hacking, or co-living arrangements to reduce housing expenses.

Consider factors such as location, size, amenities, and housing affordability when evaluating housing options to optimize costs.

3. Building and Maintaining Wealth

3.1 Set Financial Goals

Define clear financial goals and objectives that align with your values, priorities, and aspirations.

Establish short-term, medium-term, and long-term goals, and develop actionable plans to achieve them over time.

3.2 Pay Yourself First

Prioritize saving and investing by automating contributions to retirement accounts, investment accounts, and emergency funds.

Pay yourself first before allocating funds to expenses, and treat savings as non-negotiable commitments to your financial future.

3.3 Practice Consistent Saving and Investing

Save and invest regularly, regardless of market conditions or economic fluctuations, to build wealth steadily over time. Set up automatic transfers or contributions to savings and investment accounts to ensure consistency and discipline in your financial habits.

3.4 Stay Disciplined and Patient

Exercise discipline and patience in your financial journey, and avoid succumbing to short-term impulses or market speculation.
Stay focused on your long-term goals, maintain a diversified portfolio, and resist the temptation to make impulsive decisions based on fear or greed.

4. Conclusion

Achieving financial independence requires discipline, determination, and a commitment to living intentionally. By embracing principles of financial independence, implementing strategies for reducing expenses and increasing savings, and focusing on building and maintaining wealth over time, individuals can create a solid foundation for financial success and achieve the freedom to live life on their own terms. Whether it's retiring early, pursuing passions, or leaving a legacy, financial independence empowers individuals to pursue their dreams and create a meaningful impact in their lives and the world around them.

Conclusion

In this comprehensive guide, we've covered essential topics and strategies to help you achieve financial success and independence. Let's recap the key points and provide encouragement and motivation to start your journey towards financial freedom. Additionally, we'll suggest some additional resources for continued learning and growth.

Key Points Recap:
Financial Independence: Financial independence is the state of having enough passive income to cover living expenses without relying on a traditional job.
Budgeting: Creating and sticking to a budget is essential for managing money effectively, reducing expenses, and increasing savings.
Investing: Invest wisely in diversified assets to build wealth over time and achieve long-term financial goals.

Debt Management: Minimize debt and prioritize debt repayment to free up cash flow and accelerate wealth accumulation.

Lifestyle Choices: Live below your means, prioritize saving and investing, and avoid lifestyle inflation to maintain financial stability.

Continuous Learning: Stay informed about personal finance principles, investment strategies, and market trends to make informed financial decisions.

Encouragement and Motivation:

Starting the journey towards financial independence may seem daunting, but remember that every step you take brings you closer to your goals. Stay focused, disciplined, and patient, and celebrate small victories along the way. Surround yourself with supportive peers, seek inspiration from success stories, and visualize the future you want to create for yourself and your loved ones. Remember that financial independence is achievable with dedication, perseverance, and a willingness to learn and adapt.

Additional Resources for Continued Learning:

Books: Explore personal finance and investment books such as "The Millionaire Next Door" by Thomas J. Stanley and William D. Danko, "The Simple Path to Wealth" by J.L. Collins, and "Rich Dad Poor Dad" by Robert T. Kiyosaki.

Podcasts: Listen to personal finance and investing podcasts such as "The Dave Ramsey Show," "The Tim Ferriss Show," and "ChooseFI" for valuable insights and inspiration.

Online Courses: Enroll in online courses or workshops on personal finance, budgeting, investing, and wealth-building platforms such as Coursera, Udemy, or Khan Academy.

Financial Advisors: Consider consulting with a certified financial planner (CFP) or financial advisor for personalized guidance and advice tailored to your specific financial situation and goals.

Online Communities: Join online forums, communities, or social media groups focused on personal finance, FIRE (Financial Independence, Retire Early), or investment topics to connect with like-minded individuals, share experiences, and learn from others' journeys.

Remember that the journey towards financial independence is unique to each individual, and there is no one-size-fits-all approach. Stay true to your values, define your own path, and embrace the journey with enthusiasm and determination. With dedication, discipline, and a commitment to lifelong learning, you can achieve financial independence and create a future of abundance, freedom, and fulfillment.

Best of luck on your journey to financial independence!

Appendices

Appendix A: Glossary of Terms

Financial Independence: The state of having enough passive income to cover living expenses without relying on a traditional job.

Budgeting: The process of creating a plan to manage income and expenses effectively.

Passive Income: Income generated from investments, rental properties, or business ventures that does not require active involvement.

Asset Allocation: The distribution of investments across different asset classes such as stocks, bonds, and real estate to achieve diversification.

Compound Interest: Interest calculated on the initial principal and accumulated interest from previous periods, resulting in exponential growth over time.

Net Worth: The difference between assets and liabilities, representing an individual's overall financial position.

Diversification: Spreading investments across various assets to reduce risk and optimize returns.

Retirement Planning: The process of setting financial goals and strategies to ensure financial security during retirement years.

Emergency Fund: A savings account set aside to cover unexpected expenses or financial emergencies.

Debt Snowball: A debt repayment strategy that involves paying off debts from smallest to largest balance while making minimum payments on other debts.

Debt Avalanche: A debt repayment strategy that involves paying off debts with the highest interest rates first while making minimum payments on other debts.

Asset Allocation: The distribution of investments across different asset classes such as stocks, bonds, and real estate to achieve diversification.

Compound Interest: Interest calculated on the initial principal and accumulated interest from previous periods, resulting in exponential growth over time.

Net Worth: The difference between assets and liabilities, representing an individual's overall financial position.

401(k): A retirement savings plan offered by employers that allows employees to contribute a portion of their pre-tax income, with potential employer matching contributions.

Appendix B: Recommended Reading and Resources

Books:

"The Millionaire Next Door" by Thomas J. Stanley and William D. Danko
"The Simple Path to Wealth" by J.L. Collins
"Rich Dad Poor Dad" by Robert T. Kiyosaki
"Your Money or Your Life" by Vicki Robin and Joe Dominguez

Podcasts:

"The Dave Ramsey Show"
"The Tim Ferriss Show"
"ChooseFI"

Online Courses:

Coursera: Personal Finance, Investing, and Wealth Management courses
Udemy: Budgeting, Financial Planning, and Investment courses
Khan Academy: Personal Finance and Economics tutorials

Websites and Blogs:

Investopedia: Comprehensive resource for financial education and investment research

The Motley Fool: Stock market analysis, investment advice, and personal finance articles

Mr. Money Mustache: Blog focused on financial independence, frugality, and lifestyle design

Financial Tools and Apps:

Mint: Personal finance app for budgeting, expense tracking, and financial goal setting

YNAB (You Need a Budget): Budgeting software with emphasis on zero-based budgeting and financial accountability

Personal Capital: Investment management platform with tools for tracking net worth, retirement planning, and portfolio analysis

These resources provide valuable insights, education, and tools to support your journey towards financial independence and success. Continuously seek knowledge, stay informed, and take proactive steps to improve your financial well-being.

www.ingramcontent.com/pod-product-compliance
Lightning Source LLC
Chambersburg PA
CBHW050059230526
45470CB00004B/1597